Pasta Salads!

by Susan Janine Meyer

Specialty Cookbook Series Edited by Andrea Chesman

The Crossing Press, Trumansburg, NY 14886

The following recipes were developed at Auntie Pasta, a specialty food chain located in the San Fransisco Bay Area, and are reprinted here with permission and grateful acknowledgement: Spiced Orzo Salad, Pesto Pasta Salad, Chicken Almond Curry Pasta Salad, Chardonnay Vinaigrette Rotelle Salad and Chardonnay Vinaigrette, and Martini Pasta Salad and Martini Dressing. The Hot Red Pepper Pasta, Green Onion Pasta, Herb Pasta, and Tomato Pasta recipes were based on Auntie Pasta's recipes.

Cover, title page, and text design by Betsy Bayley
Cover and text illustrations by Betsy Bayley

Printed in the U.S.A.
by McNaughton & Gunn of Ann Arbor, Michigan

Library of Congress Cataloging-in-Publication Data

Meyer, Susan Janine.
Pasta salads.

Includes index.
1. Cookery (Macaroni) 2. Salads. I. Title.
TX809.M17M49 1986 641.8'22 86-4215
ISBN 0-89594-191-0
ISBN 0-89594-190-2 (pbk.)

To my mother and father

Contents

Acknowledgements

Rustridge Vineyards and Winery, where I spent many days and nights writing and cooking

Stan, Diane, and Angie, for their encouragement, constructive criticism, and willing palates

Pat and David Howell of Auntie Pasta, for the opportunity to work for them and for their interest and enthusiasm for this cookbook project

Susan Sokol, who tirelessly helped me organize and type the manuscript

Grant, for patiently teaching me how to use his word processor and for all his encouragement

George, for being a terrific cooking assistant and taster and for his helpful suggestions

Mark Lewis, for researching the Auntie Pasta archives for pasta salad recipes

Andrea Chesman, my editor, who has done an outstanding job

Preface

I made my first pasta salad in 1982 while attending the Culinary Academy in San Francisco. Later, while I was managing one of Auntie Pasta's retail pasta shops in San Francisco, I found that many customers wanted to make their own salads but couldn't find any recipes. Spurred by the interest of the customers, I decided to write a book solely about pasta salads.

These salads use pasta as their basic ingredient much like lettuce is used for green salads. Pasta is a much more versatile base than lettuce—it comes in a variety of colors and shapes and it doesn't wilt. Pasta also mixes well with other ingredients because it catches dressings and chopped vegetables and meats in its crevices and prevents them from falling to the bottom of the bowl.

Making pasta salads can be very creative and fun not only because there are plenty of differently colored, differently flavored, and differently shaped pastas available, but because a diversity of foods can be used to complement them. My purpose in this book is to show how different types of pasta can be combined with fresh herbs, vegetables, meats, spices, cheeses, and gourmet items to make tasty salads and, at the same time, attract the eye through color, shape, and texture variations.

Pasta salads have grown in popularity because of their versatility as appetizers, as accompaniments to main course dishes, and as light meals in themselves.

The following recipes have been made with fresh, natural ingredients and quality gourmet products. I have steered away from processed and refined foods and I have not relied on butter, cream, eggs, mayonnaise, or added salt to flavor these salads. In my opinion, a meal should be both tasty and healthful, and I feel that in most cases these ingredients neither enhance the flavor of pasta salads nor are they healthful.

Each of the following pasta salad recipes has been tested and several have been sold commercially through the Auntie Pasta stores. The possibilities for pasta salads are endless—these recipes can be changed according to your tastes and to the foods available.

I
All About Pasta Salads

A pasta salad can be created simply by combining freshly cooked pasta with a vegetable, some herbs, and cheese. On the other hand, it can be a very complicated combination of pasta, meat, poulty, seafood, fruits, and nuts—or it can be any combination in between. Because of the wide selection of pastas available, and the unlimited combination of ingredients that will complement them, pasta salads can be made with infinite variety.

A pasta salad usually requires a dressing, most often consisting of oil, vinegar, and perhaps some mustard and some spices, to tie the salad together and bring out its flavors. The ingredients that go into the dressing determine the overall flavor of the salad. Olive oil is the traditional oil of European, Middle Eastern, and American salads. Unfortunately, many of the olive oil products that Americans use are tasteless because they have been highly processed. Recipes from this collection are ideally made with *virgin* olive oil, the purest, most flavorful olive oil that one can purchase.

Though our Mediterranean counterparts have quietly enjoyed it for centuries, virgin olive oil first hit the mainstream American market in about 1980. It has since severely challenged the dominant pure olive oil market by converting consumers to its use after just one taste comparison. Now restaurant menus boast of their use of virgin olive oils in their appetizers and salads, while specialty stores continue to add new varieties of these oils to their shelves. At one time most imported olive oil came primarily from Italy and Spain. Now our choices include French, Greek, and even California olive oils.

Olive oil labeling can be very misleading. In the United States, the Food and Drug Administration regulates the use of the name "virgin olive oil" for oil that is produced from the first, cold pressing of the olives. A domestically produced "extra virgin olive oil" is not necessarily different or better than a "virgin olive oil." In addition, blends of refined and virgin olive oil cannot be called "virgin olive oil," but must be labeled "pure olive oil." France, Italy, and Spain have the most stringent labeling policies of all olive oil importers yet their use of the terms "extra virgin," "fine virgin," and "virgin" are based on the acid levels of the oils. Although cold-pressed olive oil generally has a low acidity, the acid level of olive oil can be lowered through the refining process. Thus, such labeling does not always insure that the contents are from the first pressing.

The palate is the best judge of the quality of olive oil. A good olive oil should have the color and taste of the olive. This olive flavor, or fruitiness, varies widely among olive oils. Because cold-pressed olive oils are characteristically fragrant and tasty, they should be used in cold or lightly sautéed dishes to be appreciated. Blended and refined oils lend themselves to general cooking because of their more neutral taste, their higher heating point, and their lower cost.

Every ingredient that goes into a pasta salad should contribute some flavor. If olive oil is used in a recipe, it should contribute an olive taste to the dish, otherwise it would be better to use another type of oil.

For some salad dressings I prefer to use a more subtle oil, such as safflower or corn oil, which won't overpower the other ingredients. This is especially true for dressings that use lemon juice or flavored vinegars. Nut oils, such as walnut oil and peanut oil, also lend particular flavors to salads. Walnut oil has a distinctively nutty flavor, peanut oil adds a hint of oriental flavor to the salad. In oriental-style salads, dark sesame oil is a key ingredient because it imparts that characteristic flavor we have come to recognize in oriental cooking.

Vinegars also can contribute to the flavor of pasta salads. While they generally provide the needed astringency, or bite, to a salad, they can add more than acidity to the salad. There are several varieties of wine vinegar that add unique flavors and complexity to salads.

Wine vinegar is a natural food that results from the action of a bacteria indigenous to wine. This bacteria, when it is exposed to air, converts the alcohol in the wine to acetic acid, or vinegar. Ordinary wine vinegar is made from red or white table wine. A varietal wine vinegar is made from a specific wine, such as Zinfandel or Chardonnay. It can also be made from sherry and champagne. For certain recipes, I prefer varietal wine vinegars over other wine vinegars for their distinct flavors. Varietal wine vinegars usually can be purchased at specialty food shops and large supermarkets.

Italy has its own version of wine vinegar, the exceptional *aceto balsamico*. Balsamic vinegar is aged in wooden barrels for at least a decade. In the process of changing to different barrels, it develops the scent of a fine wine, a mellow sweet and sour flavor, and a red-brown color. The resulting vinegar provides a special touch to marinades and salads for which there is no substitute.

In addition to the familiar vegetables, cheeses, and meats that I have used in the pasta salad recipes, I have included a wide range of gourmet foods and some less common vegetables, herbs, and spices. Because some of these items may be new to you, I have compiled a glossary of ethnic foods and seasonings at the end of the book.

Pasta salads are an excellent medium for trying out new products. Take this opportunity to expand your knowledge of the foods that are available.

Pasta

From the large variety of pasta shapes that are available, I have chosen the 16 shapes I feel are best suited to pasta salads.

Shape	Description
Creste de gallo, or rooster's comb	A tubular pasta with a fluted edge
Fusilli, commonly called corkscrew pasta, or rotelle	A thick, tightly coiled pasta
Small shells, about ½-inch long	They look like sea shells
Medium shells, about 1-inch long	Some varieties look like sea shells, others look more like snail shells
Cavatappi or fusilli col buco	They look like fusilli but are loosely coiled and tubular
Gnocci	Similar to shells, but they look somewhat like the famed Italian dumpling by the same name
Orzo or rosamarina	It looks like long-grain rice
Wagon wheels	Miniature wheels with spokes
Bowties or farfalle	Americans think they look like bowties, but the Italians call them butterflies

Rigatoni or macaroni	Tubular pasta, some are fat and short, others are long and thin, some are bent. I do not distinguish between the many different varieties. Use the ones you like best!
Spaghetti rings	They look like wagon wheels without the spokes
Penne or mostaciolli	Similar to rigatoni but their ends are cut off at angles
Capellini or angels' hair	Extremely thin, long strands of pasta
Spaghetti or tagliarini	Thin, long strands that can be round or flat
Linguine	Long flat noodles, usually about 1/8-inch wide
Fettuccine	Long flat noodles, 1/4-3/8-inch wide

When I choose a certain pasta shape for a salad, I have several considerations in mind. First I consider the salad theme. For the Tex-Mex Wagon Wheel Salad, for example, I chose wagon wheels because they remind me of the Old West. In the Louisiana Orzo Salad, I chose orzo because I was creating a jambalaya-type dish, which is traditionally made of rice. In several seafood pasta salads I use shells.

I also consider the ability of the pasta to hold the other ingredients. In the Broccoli and Prawn Linguine Salad, I chose linguine because the long thin strands make a netting that keeps the broccoli and prawns from falling to the bottom of the plate. In addition, the fresh herbs stick to the flat surface of the noodles, whereas they might slide off round noodles. In the Florets and Cherry Tomato Gnocci Salad I chose gnocci or shells because they can catch the broccoli, cauliflower, and tomatoes in their crevices, preventing them from all falling to the bottom of the bowl.

Eye appeal is always important. The Brunch Pasta Salad has square, round, thick, and thin ingredients, so I added a long tubular pasta to enhance the variety of the salad. The Greek Feta Bowtie Salad has a variety of colors, and it needed a background to show them off, so I chose the bowties which serve as miniature plates that display the colorful ingredients.

My choices of shapes may not agree with yours, but there is plenty of room for imagination, so substitute pasta shapes as you see fit.

In general I use a single type of pasta per salad. I have seen pasta salads that combined several shapes in a single salad. This is easy to do when you make a large quantity. If you make a pasta salad for only 4–6 people, you may not want to boil 3 separate batches of pasta consisting of 4 ounces each. Nevertheless, a buffet salad that contains shells, fusilli, and bowties can be quite interesting.

What are the Differences Between Fresh and Dry Pasta?

Fresh pasta is a fairly recent arrival to the American marketplace; dry pasta has been around seemingly forever. Although many dry pastas are of excellent quality, fresh pasta is in greater demand and is considered better. But aside from minor differences in taste, fresh pasta is not necessarily the optimum choice for all pasta dishes.

More variety in shapes is possible with dry pasta. With fresh pasta, you are limited to long, flat or round noodles, shells, and fusilli. On the other hand, fresh pasta can be made in an almost infinite variety of flavors and colors. Dry pasta is pretty much limited to egg and spinach flavors, although others are becoming available.

Dry pasta is firm and highly resilient while fresh pasta is delicate and tends to get sticky. Fresh pasta cooks in 15 to 120 seconds, depending on its thickness, while dry pasta will take 2 to 10 minutes, depending on its size. Dry pasta expands 80 to 95 percent when it is cooked, while fresh pasta expands only 10 to 12 percent.

Dry pasta will keep for several months. If wrapped in plastic, fresh pasta will keep up to 1 week in the refrigerator or up to 1 month in the freezer.

In the following pasta salad recipes, I have used dry pasta more often than fresh mainly because of the variety of shapes to choose from, its hardiness, and its long shelf life. I frequently use fresh pasta in delicate pasta salads because it has a lighter texture than dry pasta. I also use fresh pasta when I want to add certain colors or flavors to the salad that are not provided by dry pastas. If fresh pasta is available to you, try some and compare it with the dry products that you are used to, or make your own!

Cooking Pasta

The best piece of equipment to use to cook pasta is a large pot with a colander insert. With this device the pasta cooks inside the colander, which can be pulled out of the boiling water instantly, preventing the possibility of overcooking. Be sure to cook the pasta in plenty of boiling water, at least 4 quarts of water to 1 pound of pasta. Add a few drops of oil to the boiling water to keep the pasta from sticking together and to prevent the water from boiling over.

Pasta salad noodles must be cooked *al dente* (until tender but firm) because they tend to soften when marinated with the other ingredients. Remember that fresh pasta cooks quickly, so be sure to follow the directions of the salesperson; do not cook more than 2 minutes. Dry pasta can be tasted periodically while it is cooking to determine when it is done. It is best not to rely on package instructions because they usually do not apply to pasta salads.

As soon as the pasta is cooked, rinse it thoroughly in cold water to prevent further cooking. (Rinsing the pasta will also remove the starchy coating from the noodles and prevent them from sticking together.)

Then shake out the excess water from the pasta and transfer it from the colander to a large mixing bowl. Depending on the recipe, toss the pasta with salad oil or salad dressing. The pasta is now ready to provide the base for a pasta salad.

Making, Garnishing, and Serving Pasta Salads

Making a salad look attractive is one of the most important tasks of the cook. Many a wonderful salad has been passed over on a buffet table because it didn't look appetizing. In order to create an attractive and tasty salad, care must be taken in its construction. For example, fresh herbs, parsley, garlic, and spices should be mixed directly with the freshly cooked pasta or with the salad dressing. This will allow their flavors to be absorbed and distributed evenly. Durable foods, such as meats, raw vegetables, and nuts, should be tossed with the pasta before less durable items, such as cooked vegetables. Delicate foods should always be added last and should be tossed as little as possible to prevent damaging them.

The salad dressing should be tossed with the pasta salad either before or after adding all the other ingredients except the most delicate ones, like soft cheeses and fresh tomatoes. If the dressing has a thick consistency, for example a pesto or honey sesame dressing, then it is better to coat the noodles with the dressing before adding any other ingredients. Sometimes adding the dressing directly to the pasta will allow the flavor to be better distributed throughout the salad.

Present your salads in bowls and platters that are fitting to the salad. If the salad has a lot of variety to it, choose a plain bowl or serving dish; if it is a simple salad, use a more ornate serving dish. Instead of serving the salad in a large bowl, you may want to place the pasta on individual plates. In this case, you might mound the salad on a bed of lettuce or spinach, or in an avocado boat or in a hollowed-out tomato. Be creative! Reserve enough fresh herbs, parsley, or other colorful ingredients from the salad to garnish the center and edges of the salad before serving it.

Pasta salads should be served when they are freshest, but they can be made ahead of time because they keep well in the refrigerator up to a couple of days. Store the dressing, fragile ingredients, and the garnish separately, and add to the salad just before serving.

Unless otherwise stated in the recipe, it is best not to serve the pasta salad directly out of the refrigerator, because the flavors of the ingredients will be subdued and the pasta will have a sticky texture. For maximum flavor and texture, I generally serve pasta salads at room temperature.

Recipe Yields

The recipes in this text are geared for between 4 and 12 servings. These portions are based on how many other ingredients are mixed with the pasta and how the salad is served. Some salads work well as main courses and will provide 4–6 portions. Others work better as side dishes and can serve as few as 6 or as many as 12. Each recipe contains slightly under 1 pound of cooked pasta. Because uncooked fresh pasta and dry pasta of equal weight vary considerably in quantity when cooked, I have adjusted each recipe to use either ¾ pound of uncooked fresh pasta or ½ pound of uncooked dry pasta. These uncooked weights will both yield approximately 1 pound of cooked pasta.

2
Homemade Pastas

Making your own fresh pasta can be very satisfying. The process takes surprisingly little time—and it is fun to do. The combination of just-made homemade pasta and crispy young vegetables creates a salad unparalleled in flavor and freshness.

Unbleached all-purpose flour or semolina flour can be used to make pasta. Semolina makes a more dense, yellow pasta and is the flour used in most Italian pastas and in fresh pastas. I recommend using a food processor with the semolina flour because its grainy texture makes it hard to handle otherwise. Rice flour, which can be purchased in health food stores and oriental markets, is an ideal flour to sprinkle over pasta because its coarse cornmeal-like texture helps to prevent the fresh noodles from sticking together as they are rolled and cut. If rice flour is unavailable, use all-purpose flour instead.

Basic Egg Pasta

1½ cups unbleached all-purpose or semolina flour
2 large eggs
1 tablespoon vegetable oil
Rice flour

Yield: ¾ pound fresh pasta

Mixing the Dough by Hand

Put the flour on a wooden board or countertop. Make a well in the flour and break the eggs into it. Add the oil and gently beat the eggs with a fork while slowly combining the flour with the eggs. Continue stirring until the eggs and the flour are fairly well combined. The mixture will be too stiff to continue mixing with a fork. Gently knead in the rest of the flour with your hands for several minutes. It will be more difficult to knead than bread dough. Let the dough rest covered in plastic wrap for at least 30 minutes.

Mixing the Dough by Electric Mixer

Use the paddle attachment. Put the flour, eggs, and oil in the bowl and turn on the beater. After about 1 minute, the dough will have a coarse, crumbly consistency. Replace the paddle with the dough hook and knead the pasta for about 5 minutes. Remove it from the bowl and let it rest covered in plastic wrap for at least 30 minutes.

Mixing the Dough in a Food Processor

This is my favorite method. Use the metal blade. Add the flour to the bowl and turn the motor on. Add the eggs and oil through the feed tube. Let the machine run until the dough forms a ball. If it is too sticky, add more flour and process briefly. If it is too dry, add a few drops of water. Knead the dough on a floured surface for 3–5 minutes or until it becomes a smooth ball. Let it rest covered in plastic wrap for at least 30 minutes.

Mixing the Dough in an Extruder Machine

If you have an extruder machine, be sure to follow the directions of the manufacturer.

Rolling Out the Dough

I do not recommend hand rolling the dough unless you are skilled with a rolling pin. It will be considerably easier to use a roller-type pasta machine, a relatively modest and worthwhile investment, if you plan to make pasta more than once. This machine comes in both automatic and manual styles, but I prefer to use the manual pasta machine because it almost necessitates that I work with a helper, which I find adds to the enjoyment of making pasta.

Once the dough has rested, divide it into about 4 pieces. Rewrap 3 pieces in plastic. Flatten the fourth piece with your hand so that it will fit through the pasta machine at its widest setting. Feed the pasta into the rollers with one hand while cranking the machine with the other hand. As soon as the roller begins to take the dough, get ready to catch it as it comes out of the rollers. This is where the second person comes in handy. If the pasta has ragged edges or holes in it, reshape it, fold it over, and feed it through the rollers again.

When the dough becomes smooth and elastic, begin narrowing the opening between the rollers and continue thinning out the dough until it achieves the thickness that you want. (As the pasta gets thinner, the strip gets longer so be sure to cut it into smaller more manageable pieces before inserting them through the rollers again.)

When the pasta sheet is at the thickness that you want, lay it flat on a well-floured board or sheet pan. Use rice flour if possible. Sprinkle the exposed side with flour also. Do not layer the pasta sheets on top of each other because they will stick together. Let the pasta dry out a bit while you finish rolling out the other pieces of dough. Do not let the pasta become brittle or it will crumble in the pasta cutter. Cover it with a dish towel if it starts to get too dry to handle.

Affix the desired cutting attachment to the pasta machine and adjust the hand crank if necessary so that it spins the roller of the cutter. Feed the pasta strips into the cutter and make sure you catch the pasta ribbons before they fall into a pile at the base of the machine. Douse the freshly cut pasta in the rice flour and loop them loosely around your fingers to make a nest.

At this point you have several choices: You can let the pasta dry on a rack or tray, you can keep it fresh by putting it in a plastic bag in the refrigerator, you can freeze it in a plastic bag, or you can toss it immediately into boiling water.

For maximum flavor I suggest using the fresh pasta as soon as possible. Dried pasta will keep for several months; fresh pasta will keep for up to 1 week in the refrigerator; frozen pasta will keep well for up to 1 month in the freezer. If you decide to freeze the pasta, do not thaw it, transfer it directly from the freezer to the boiling water and add 30 seconds to its cooking time.

The following recipes for flavored pastas can be messy to make by hand so I recommend using an electric mixer or food processor.

Spinach Pasta

1½ cups unbleached all-purpose or semolina flour
½ pound fresh spinach, wilted and squeezed dry, or 5 ounces frozen spinach, defrosted and squeezed dry
1 large egg
1 tablespoon vegetable oil

Yield: ¾ pound fresh pasta

Try spinach pasta in the Ceviche Pasta Salad (pages 94–95) or the Chicken Almond Curry Pasta Salad (page 105).

Mix the flour with the spinach before adding the other ingredients to the bowl of a food processor or electric mixer. Mix and knead the dough, let it rest, roll it out, and cut the pasta to size according to the directions on pages 23–26.

Beet Pasta

1½ cups unbleached all-purpose or semolina flour
2–3 tablespoons grated cooked or canned beets
2 large eggs
1 tablespoon vegetable oil

Yield: ¾ pound fresh pasta

Try this pasta in the Slavic Macaroni Salad (pages 126–27).

Add the flour, beets, eggs, and oil to the bowl of a food processor or electric mixer. The more beets you use, the redder the pasta will be. Mix and knead the dough, let it rest, roll it out, and cut the pasta to size according to the directions on pages 23–26.

Tomato Pasta

1¾ cups unbleached all-purpose or semolina flour
2 tablespoons tomato paste
1 large egg
1 tablespoon vegetable oil

Yield: ¾ pound fresh pasta

Use this pasta in salads that contain tomatoes, such as the Fresh Tomato Fusilli Salad (pages 62–63). The pasta has an orange-red color.

Add the flour, tomato paste, egg, and oil to the bowl of a food processor or electric mixer. Mix and knead the dough, let it rest, roll it out, and cut the pasta to size according to the directions on pages 23–26.

Green Onion Pasta

2–3 tablespoons sliced green onions or scallions
1½ cups unbleached all-purpose or semolina flour
2 large eggs
1 tablespoon vegetable oil

Yield: ¾ pound fresh pasta

Delicious in any pasta salad recipe that uses green onions. Try it with the Three Cheese Deli Salad (page 119).

In a food processor or blender, process the onions to a fine puree. Add to the flour with the eggs and the vegetable oil to the bowl of a food processor or electric mixer. Mix and knead the dough, let it rest, roll it out, and cut the pasta to size according to the directions on pages 23–26.

Black Pepper Pasta

2 teaspoons freshly ground black pepper
1½ cups unbleached all-purpose or semolina flour
2 large eggs
1 tablespoon vegetable oil

Yield: ¾ pound fresh pasta

Substitute black pepper pasta for the orzo in the Louisiana Orzo Salad (pages 110–11). A very interesting variation!

Mix the black pepper with the flour in the bowl of a food processor or electric mixer. Then add the eggs and oil. Mix and knead the dough, let it rest, roll it out, and cut the pasta to size according to the directions on pages 23–26.

Garlic Pasta

5–6 garlic cloves
1–2 tablespoons water
2 large eggs
1 tablespoon vegetable oil
1¾ cup unbleached all-purpose or semolina flour

Yield: ¾ pound fresh pasta

Use in any pasta salad that requires garlic. Try it with the Pesto Pasta Salad (pages 66–67).

In a food processor or blender, puree the garlic with 1–2 tablespoons of water. Combine the garlic, eggs, and oil with the flour in the bowl of a food processor or electric mixer. Mix and knead the dough, let it rest, roll it out, and cut the pasta to size according to the directions on pages 23–26.

Herb Pasta

2 tablespoons finely chopped fresh mixed herbs (basil, thyme, sage, rosemary, oregano, marjoram)
1½ cups unbleached all-purpose or semolina flour
2 large eggs
1 tablespoon vegetable oil

Yield: ¾ pound fresh pasta

This pasta is ideal for any pasta salad recipe that uses fresh herbs. Try it in the Mediterranean Pasta Salad (page 72).

Mix at least 3 types of herbs together in equal proportions. Process the herbs to a fine puree in a food processor or blender. Then mix them with the flour in the bowl of a food processor or electric mixer. Add the eggs and oil. Mix and knead the dough, let it rest, roll it out, and cut the pasta to size according to the directions on pages 23–26.

Variation

Basil Pasta. Substitute ½ cup tightly packed basil leaves for the fresh herbs. Process to a fine puree before adding to the flour. Proceed with the recipe above.

Lemon Pasta

Rind of 1 lemon, finely grated
1¾ cups unbleached all-purpose or semolina flour
¼ cup fresh lemon juice
1 large egg
1 tablespoon vegetable oil

Yield: ¾ pound fresh pasta

This pasta is excellent with seafood, vegetable, and fruit pasta salads. Try it with the Dessert Pasta Salad (page 84).

Mix the rind with the flour in the bowl of a food processor or electric mixer before adding the other ingredients. Add the lemon juice with the egg and oil. Mix and knead the dough, let it rest, roll it out, and cut the pasta to size according to the directions on pages 23–26.

Hot Red Pepper Pasta

2 teaspoons dried hot red pepper flakes
1½ cups unbleached all-purpose or semolina flour
2 large eggs
1 tablespoon vegetable oil

Yield: ¾ pound fresh pasta

This pasta adds a wonderful hot flavor to any pasta dish. Try it with the Chicken Almond Curry Pasta Salad (page 105) or the Hunan Ginger Chicken Pasta Salad (page 108).

Mix the hot pepper flakes with the flour in the bowl of a food processor or electric mixer. Then add the eggs and oil. Mix and knead the dough, let it rest, roll it out, and cut the pasta to size according to the directions on pages 23–26.

Whole Wheat Pasta

1 cup whole wheat flour
¼ cup unbleached all-purpose flour
2 large eggs
1 tablespoon vegetable oil

Yield: ¾ pound fresh pasta

Try this pasta in the Whole Wheat Health Salad (page 83) and the Oriental Noodle Salad (page 109).

Mix the whole wheat flour with the white flour in the bowl of a food processor or electric mixer. Then add the eggs and oil. Mix and knead the dough, let it rest, roll it out, and cut the pasta to size according to the directions on pages 23–26.

3
Pasta Salad Dressings

Italian Dressing

1½ tablespoons red wine vinegar
1½ tablespoons white wine vinegar
1 garlic clove, minced
½ teaspoon minced capers
3 tablespoons virgin olive oil
Freshly ground black pepper

Yield: About ⅓ cup

In a small bowl, whisk the red and white wine vinegars with the garlic and capers. Slowly add the olive oil, continuing to stir. Add enough olive oil to achieve a good acid balance. Grind the black pepper into the dressing to taste. Shake well or whisk briefly before adding to a salad.

French Dressing

1 tablespoon white wine vinegar
1 teaspoon Dijon-style mustard
3 tablespoons virgin olive oil

Yield: About ¼ cup

In a small bowl, whisk together the vinegar and mustard. Slowly add the olive oil while stirring the mixture until the olive oil is well combined. Whisk again briefly before adding to a salad.

Vinaigrette

¼ cup virgin olive oil
2 tablespoons red or white wine vinegar
Freshly ground black pepper

In a small bowl, whisk the oil into the vinegar. Add black pepper to taste. Whisk again briefly before adding to a salad.

Yield: About ⅓ cup

Caper Vinaigrette

2 teaspoons white wine vinegar
2 teaspoons lemon juice
2 teaspoons chopped fresh parsley
1 teaspoon minced capers
¼ cup virgin olive oil
Freshly ground black pepper

Yield: About ⅓ cup

In a small bowl, whisk the vinegar with the lemon juice, parsley, and capers. Drizzle the olive oil into the mixture while whisking it. When well combined, add black pepper to taste. Whisk again briefly before adding to a salad.

Balsamic Vinaigrette

1 tablespoon balsamic vinegar
1 garlic clove, minced
1 tablespoon Dijon-style mustard
3 tablespoons virgin olive oil
Freshly ground black pepper

In a small bowl, whisk the vinegar with the garlic and mustard. Continue to whisk the dressing while slowly adding the olive oil. Add black pepper to taste. Whisk again briefly before adding to a salad.

Yield: About ¼ cup

Lemon Vinaigrette

2 tablespoons lemon juice
1 teaspoon Dijon-style mustard
¼ teaspoon sugar
¼ cup light vegetable oil
Freshly ground black pepper

Yield: About ⅓ cup

In a small bowl, whisk the lemon juice with the mustard. Add the sugar and mix well. Add the vegetable oil gradually while continuing to whisk. Add black pepper to taste. Whisk again briefly before adding to a salad.

Chardonnay Vinaigrette

2 tablespoons Chardonnay vinegar
¼ cup virgin olive oil
2 teaspoons finely chopped mixed herbs (marjoram, rosemary, basil, oregano)

Yield: About ⅓ cup

In a small bowl, whisk the vinegar with the olive oil. Add a combination of 2 or more of the fresh herbs to the dressing. Stir or shake well to distribute the flavors of the herbs into the dressing. Stir or shake again briefly before adding to a salad.

Raspberry Walnut Vinaigrette

¼ cup raspberry vinegar
2 tablespoons minced shallots
2 tablespoons minced fresh parsley
¼ cup finely chopped walnuts
2 tablespoons walnut oil

Yield: About ½ cup

In a small bowl, whisk the vinegar, shallots, parsley, and walnuts together. Gradually stir in the oil. Shake well or whisk again briefly before tossing with the salad.

Martini Dressing

1 tablespoon white wine vinegar
2 garlic cloves, minced
1 tablespoon finely chopped fresh basil or basil preserved in olive oil
3 tablespoons virgin olive oil
1–2 tablespoons Romano cheese

Yield: About ¼ cup

In a small bowl, whisk the vinegar with the garlic and basil. Add the oil gradually and whisk to combine with the other ingredients. Fold in the cheese. Whisk again briefly before adding to a salad.

Note

To preserve fresh basil, chop it finely and mix it with enough olive oil to make a paste. The basil should keep for several months in the refrigerator in a covered container. The basil leaves will turn brown but this will not affect its flavor.

Lemon-Herb Dressing

2 tablespoons fresh lemon juice
2 garlic cloves, minced
1–2 tablespoons fresh marjoram or oregano
2 tablespoons virgin olive oil
Freshly ground black pepper

Yield: About ¼ cup

In a small bowl, whisk the lemon juice with the garlic and herbs. Slowly whisk in the oil. Add black pepper to taste. Whisk again briefly before adding to a salad.

Lemon-Dill Dressing

2 tablespoons fresh lemon juice
1 garlic clove, minced
¼ cup finely chopped fresh parsley
2 teaspoons minced shallots
3 tablespoons chopped fresh dill
¼ cup vegetable oil
Freshly ground black pepper

Yield: About ½ cup

In a small bowl, whisk the lemon juice with the garlic, parsley, shallots, and dill. Gradually add the oil and mix the dressing well to combine all the ingredients. Add black pepper to taste. Whisk again briefly before adding to a salad.

Mustard-Dill Dressing

1 tablespoon red wine vinegar
1 tablespoon Dijon-style mustard
2 tablespoons virgin olive oil
1 tablespoon chopped fresh dill
Freshly ground black pepper

In a small bowl, whisk the vinegar and mustard together. Slowly whisk in the olive oil. Add the fresh dill and black pepper to taste. Whisk again briefly or shake well before adding to the salad.

Yield: About ¼ cup

Hot Mustard Dressing

2 tablespoons white wine vinegar
2 teaspoons prepared hot mustard
¼ cup virgin olive oil
1 tablespoon finely chopped fresh basil

Yield: About ⅓ cup

In a small bowl, whisk the vinegar with the mustard. Gradually add the olive oil and continue to whisk until well combined. Then whisk the fresh basil into the dressing. Use at once or store tightly covered. Hot mustard loses its punch when exposed to air.

Oriental Sesame Dressing

2 tablespoons rice wine vinegar
1 tablespoon dry sherry
1 tablespoon soy sauce
1 teaspoon sugar
1 tablespoon sesame oil
1 teaspoon sesame seeds

Yield: About ⅓ cup

In a small bowl, whisk the vinegar with the sherry, soy sauce, and sugar. Add the sesame oil and stir well to combine. Fold the sesame seeds into the dressing. Whisk again briefly before adding to a salad.

Hunan Dressing

1 tablespoon rice wine vinegar
1 tablespoon soy sauce
1 teaspoon sugar
2 tablespoons sesame oil
1 tablespoon chili oil
1 garlic clove, minced
1 tablespoon minced ginger root or 1 tablespoon ginger juice (squeezed from fresh ginger root with a garlic press)

Yield: About ⅓ cup

In a small bowl, whisk the vinegar with the soy sauce and sugar. Add the sesame oil and chili oil and mix well. Add the garlic and ginger. Let the dressing marinate for about 15 minutes before using. Whisk briefly before adding to a salad.

Orange-Ginger-Soy Dressing

½ cup fresh orange juice
2 tablespoons sesame oil
2 tablespoons soy sauce
1 tablespoon finely chopped fresh ginger root or 1 tablespoon ginger juice (squeezed from fresh ginger root with a garlic press)

Yield: ¾ cup

In a small bowl, whisk the orange juice with the sesame oil, soy sauce, and the ginger. Whisk again briefly before adding the dressing to a salad.

Tex-Mex Dressing

1 tablespoon white wine vinegar
2 teaspoons lime juice
½ teaspoon dry mustard or Dijon-style prepared mustard
1 garlic clove, minced
½ teaspoon cayenne pepper
3 tablespoons safflower oil
1½ teaspoons finely chopped fresh cilantro

Yield: About ⅓ cup

In a small bowl, whisk the vinegar with the lime juice, mustard, garlic, and cayenne. Add the oil gradually while continuing to whisk. Fold in the cilantro. Whisk briefly before adding to a salad.

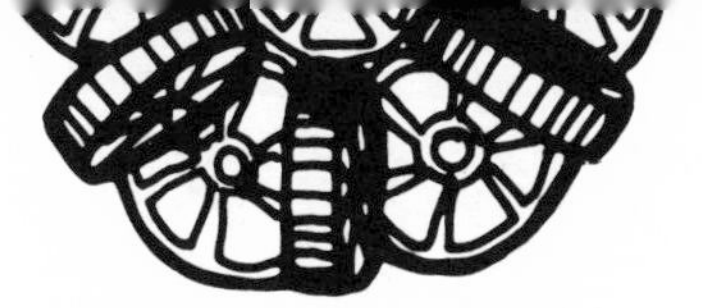

New Orleans Dressing

3 tablespoons white wine vinegar
2 teaspoons lemon juice
2 teaspoons Dijon-style mustard
½ teaspoon cayenne pepper
1 tablespoon finely chopped fresh parsley
1 tablespoon fresh thyme leaves
5 tablespoons vegetable oil
Tabasco sauce
Freshly ground black pepper

Yield: About ⅔ cup

In a small bowl, whisk the vinegar with the lemon juice and mustard. Add the cayenne, parsley, and thyme. Gradually whisk the oil into the dressing. Add the Tabasco and black pepper to taste. Whisk or stir briefly before adding to a salad.

Horseradish Dressing

1 tablespoon prepared horseradish or freshly grated horseradish mixed with vinegar
1 tablespoon sour cream
1 tablespoon virgin olive oil
1 tablespoon red wine vinegar
Freshly ground black pepper

Yield: About ¼ cup

In a small bowl, whisk the horseradish with the sour cream and olive oil. Add the vinegar and black pepper to taste and stir well before adding to a salad.

4
Meatless Pasta Salads

Summer Vegetable Bowtie Salad

½ pound dry bowties
1 tablespoon virgin olive oil
2–3 medium-size carrots
¼–⅓ pound fresh or frozen green beans
½–¾ cup fresh or frozen corn kernels
½ cup fresh or frozen peas
⅓ cup Vinaigrette Dressing (page 40)
¼ cup chopped fresh parsley
1 tablespoon fresh thyme leaves
¼–⅓ cup freshly grated Parmigiano-Reggiano cheese

Yield: 8–10 side dish servings

Fresh vegetables make a lovely salad, especially if you can harvest them from your own garden.

Cook the pasta in boiling water until *al dente*. Rinse in cold water and drain. Transfer to a serving bowl and toss with the olive oil.

Slice the carrots on the diagonal into ¼-inch-thick slices. Blanch in boiling water until just tender crisp, 2–3 minutes. Refresh in cold water to stop further cooking.

Slice fresh green beans on the diagonal into 1½-inch pieces and blanch in boiling water for 1–2 minutes. Refresh in cold water to stop further cooking, then drain. Do not blanch frozen beans.

If the corn is tender and sweet, or if it is frozen, it will not need to be blanched.

Otherwise place the corn in a small strainer and blanch in boiling water for about 30 seconds. Refresh in cold water and drain.

Add the carrots, beans, corn, and peas to the pasta. Make the dressing and combine it with the parsley and thyme. Add the dressing to the salad and mix well. Sprinkle the cheese on top and serve.

Miniature Vegetable Pasta Salad

¾ pound fresh egg fettuccine (pages 23–26) or herb fettuccine (page 33)
1 tablespoon virgin olive oil
4–6 whole miniature zucchini, about 4 inches long
4–6 whole miniature crookneck squash, about 4 inches long
4–6 whole baby corn
¼ cup Balsamic Vinaigrette (page 42)
1 cup cherry tomatoes, halved
⅓–½ cup freshly grated Parmesan cheese
Thinly sliced fresh chives

Yield: 4–6 servings

Cook the pasta in boiling water until *al dente*. Rinse in cold water, drain. Transfer to a serving platter and toss with the olive oil.

Blanch whole zucchini and crookneck squash in boiling water for 3–5 minutes, or until tender but crisp. Refresh in cold water to stop further cooking, drain, and halve lengthwise.

If the baby corn is fresh, blanch it in boiling water for 1 minute, refresh in cold water, and drain. If it is canned, rinse it well in cold water to remove the excess salt. Cut the corn into 1½-inch pieces.

Add the zucchini, crookneck squash, corn, and the dressing to the pasta and toss well. Fold in the tomatoes. Sprinkle the cheese over the salad. Garnish the salad with the chives and serve.

Macaroni Salad

½ pound dry macaroni (multi-flavored macaroni is best)
1 tablespoon virgin olive oil
1 cup finely sliced celery
4 ounces pimientos, drained and diced
2 tablespoons finely chopped red onion
3–4 tablespoons thinly sliced scallions
2–3 tablespoons finely chopped fresh parsley
2 garlic cloves, minced
2 fresh or canned green chiles, drained and finely chopped
¼ cup Mustard Dill Dressing (page 49)
Thinly sliced fresh chives

Yield: 8–10 servings

I believe that the macaroni salad is the original pasta salad. It has been a popular picnic item for generations. In this variation, the ingredients are fairly standard except for the substitution of a creamy mustard-dill sauce for the traditional mayonnaise.

Cook the pasta in plenty of boiling water until *al dente*. Rinse in cold water, drain. Transfer to a mixing bowl and toss with the olive oil. Add the celery, pimientos, onion, scallions, parsley, garlic, and green chiles to the pasta and mix well.

Toss the salad with the dressing and garnish with the chives. Serve with other picnic foods.

Fresh Tomato Fusilli Salad

1 garlic clove
½ cup tightly packed fresh basil leaves
½ cup virgin olive oil
4 large tomatoes
Freshly ground black pepper
½ pound dry egg fusilli
6–8 Greek olives, quartered (optional)
¼–⅓ cup freshly grated Parmigiano-Reggiano cheese (optional)

Yield: 6–8 servings

This salad is very light and refreshing and is best served chilled. If possible, serve the salad with slices of fresh Italian buffalo mozzarella.

In a blender or food processor, process the garlic until pureed. Add the basil and process until finely chopped. Then add the oil and blend until well combined.

Score, then blanch the tomatoes in boiling water for 30 seconds to loosen the skins. Peel, halve, and seed the tomatoes under running water. Pat dry and chop into bite-size pieces. Transfer to a medium-size bowl. Add the basil mixture to the tomatoes and grind black pepper to taste over the tomatoes. Chill for about 1 hour.

Cook the pasta in boiling water until *al dente*, rinse in cold water, and drain.

Transfer to a serving bowl.

Add the tomato mixture to the pasta and toss gently. If desired, mix in the olives and sprinkle the salad with the cheese. Garnish the salad with fresh basil leaves and serve immediately.

Florets & Cherry Tomato Gnocci Salad

½ pound dry gnocci or ½ pound dry medium shells
1 tablespoon virgin olive oil
2 cups broccoli florets
2 cups cauliflower florets
⅓ cup Hot Mustard Dressing (page 51)
1 cup cherry tomatoes, halved
⅓–½ cup Parmesan cheese

Yield: 8–10 side dish servings

Cook the pasta in boiling water until *al dente*, rinse in cold water, and drain. Transfer to a serving bowl and toss with the olive oil.

Steam the broccoli and cauliflower florets together for 5–7 minutes, or until just tender-crisp. Refresh in cold water to stop further cooking, drain, and cut into bite-size pieces.

Add the florets to the pasta. Then add the dressing and toss well. Add the tomatoes and mix gently. Sprinkle the salad with the cheese and serve.

Tex-Mex Wagon Wheel Salad

½ pound dry wagon wheels
1 tablespoon safflower oil
2 medium-size firm tomatoes
¼ pound cheddar cheese
¼ pound Monterey Jack cheese
2 tablespoons chopped fresh California or Anaheim green chile pepper
1 tablespoon chopped fresh jalapeño pepper
¼ cup thinly sliced black olives
2 teaspoons fresh cilantro leaves
⅓ cup Tex-Mex Dressing (page 54)
Whole olives
Cilantro leaves

Yield: 4–6 servings

This recipe uses popular ingredients from the American Southwest.

Cook the pasta in boiling water until *al dente*, rinse in cold water, and drain. Transfer to a serving bowl and toss with the safflower oil.

Score, then blanch the tomatoes in boiling water for 30 seconds to loosen the skins. Peel, halve, and seed the tomatoes under running water. Pat dry and chop into bite-size pieces.

Cut the cheeses into ¼-inch cubes.

Add the cheeses, chiles, sliced olives, and 2 teaspoons cilantro to the pasta. Add the dressing and toss well. Gently fold in the tomatoes. Garnish with whole olives and the remaining cilantro leaves and serve.

Pesto Pasta Salad

Pesto

2 large garlic cloves
2 cups fresh basil leaves
⅔ cup virgin olive oil
¾ cup freshly grated Parmesan and Pecorino Romano (mixed half and half)

Salad

¼ pound dry medium shells
¼ pound dry small shells
1 tablespoon virgin olive oil
½–¾ cup roasted red peppers, coarsely chopped
⅓ cup pine nuts or chopped walnuts (optional)
Fresh basil leaves or nuts

Yield: 6–8 servings

Pesto is a versatile sauce for pasta salads and mixes well with a variety of vegetables, with poultry, and with fish. This recipe yields about 1 cup of pesto.

The best way to make pesto is in a food processor or blender. Begin by processing the garlic. When the garlic is pureed, add the basil and ⅔ cup olive oil and continue processing until it becomes a thick paste. Add the cheese and process only until combined. Transfer the pesto to a small bowl and pour a thin layer of olive oil over it to prevent it from turning brown.

Cook the medium and small shells separately, in boiling water, until *al dente*. Rinse in cold water and drain. Combine both pastas in a mixing bowl and toss with the remaining 1 tablespoon olive oil.

Add the pesto to the pasta shells and mix well. Add the peppers and nuts to the salad and mix gently. Transfer to a serving dish. Garnish the salad with fresh basil leaves or nuts. Serve immediately; the pesto discolors rapidly.

Cilantro Pesto Pasta Salad

Cilantro Pesto

3 garlic cloves
2 cups cilantro (leaves only)
½ cup safflower or virgin olive oil
¼ cup pine nuts
⅓ cup Parmesan cheese

Salad

½ pound dry wagon wheels or ½ pound dry fusilli
1 tablespoon virgin olive oil
2 medium-size firm tomatoes
Cilantro
Pine nuts

Yield: 8–10 side dish servings

Cilantro pesto is a regional American version of the Italian basil pesto.

Make the pesto in a blender or food processor. First puree the garlic. Then add the cilantro leaves, ½ cup oil, nuts, and cheese, reserving some cilantro and pine nuts for a garnish. Blend until the mixture becomes a thick paste.

Cook the pasta in boiling water until *al dente*, rinse in cold water, and drain. Transfer to a mixing bowl and toss with the remaining 1 tablespoon olive oil.

Score, then blanch the tomatoes in boiling water for 30 seconds to loosen the skins. Peel, halve, and seed under running water. Pat dry and chop into ¼-inch pieces.

Add the pesto to the pasta and mix thoroughly. If it is too dry, add a few drops of oil. Transfer to a serving dish. Gently fold in the tomatoes before serving. Garnish the salad with fresh sprigs of cilantro and some pine nuts. Serve.

East Coast Fettuccine Salad

½–¾ pound cheddar cheese (New York cheddar is recommended)
3–4 tart green apples
1 lemon, halved
½ pound dry or ¾ pound fresh whole wheat fettuccine (page 36), cut in 2-inch pieces
1 tablespoon virgin olive oil
2–4 tablespoons cider vinegar
4 ounces Roquefort or blue cheese, crumbled
1 tablespoon finely chopped fresh dill

Yield: 8–10 side dish serving

This salad is an excellent starter to a wild game dinner.

Slice the cheddar into ¼-inch chunks. Slice the green apples into bite-size pieces and squeeze the lemon over them to prevent discoloring.

Cook the fettuccine in plenty of boiling water until *al dente*. Fresh fettuccine cooks in about 1 minute. Rinse in cold water and drain. Transfer to a serving dish and toss with the olive oil.

Add the cheddar cheese and apples to the pasta. Sprinkle the salad with the cider vinegar and toss well. Add the Roquefort or blue cheese. Garnish the salad with the fresh dill and serve.

Greek Feta Bowtie Salad

½ pound dry bowties
1 tablespoon virgin olive oil
2 tablespoons finely chopped fresh parsley
2 tablespoons finely chopped fresh dill
1 teaspoon fresh thyme leaves
¼ pound feta cheese
1 medium-size cucumber
1 large red bell pepper
5–6 medium-size radishes
8–10 Kalamata olives
2 teaspoons capers
1 tablespoon coarsely chopped red onion
½ cup Lemon Dill Dressing (page 48)

Yield: 8–10 side dish servings

A delicious Greek-style salad complemented with feta cheese and fresh dill.

Cook the bowties in boiling water until *al dente*. Rinse in cold water, drain. Transfer to a serving dish and toss with olive oil. Add the parsley, dill, and thyme to the pasta and mix well.

Cut the feta into ½-inch cubes. Skin the cucumber, halve lengthwise, core, and slice into ¼-inch-thick crescent-shaped pieces to yield 1 cup. Julienne slice the bell pepper. Slice the radishes paper thin. Pit and coarsely chop the olives. Add the feta cheese, cucumber, bell pepper, radishes, olives, capers, and red onion to the bowties.

Make the dressing, toss it with the salad, and serve.

Mediterranean Pasta Salad

¾ pound fresh herb linguine (page 33) or
½ pound dry fusilli
1 tablespoon virgin olive oil
½ teaspoon finely chopped garlic
1½ teaspoons finely chopped capers
2 tablespoons pine nuts
8–9 quartered Greek olives
2 tablespoons finely sliced scallions
3 tablespoons coarsely chopped roasted red peppers
¼ cup freshly grated Parmigiano-Reggiano or other imported Parmesan cheese
2 tablespoons finely chopped fresh parsley

Yield: 6–8 servings

This pasta dish makes an excellent dinner salad.

If you are using fresh linguine, boil it for approximately 45 seconds or until *al dente*. Dry pasta must cook for a few minutes. Rinse the pasta in cold water, drain, and transfer it to a large serving bowl or platter. Toss with the olive oil. Mix in the garlic and capers. Add the pine nuts, olives, scallions, and peppers, tossing the salad with each addition.

Before serving, sprinkle the salad with the cheese and parsley.

Cote d'Azur Fusilli Salad

½ pound dry egg and spinach fusilli
1 tablespoon virgin olive oil
8 sun-dried tomatoes marinated in olive oil
8–10 Kalamata olives
¼ pound chèvre (goat cheese)
2 garlic cloves, minced
2 teaspoons chopped fresh basil
2 tablespoons pine nuts
Balsamic vinegar
2 tablespoons freshly sliced chives

Yield: 8–10 side dish servings

This recipe has all those wonderful foods found in the South of France.

Cook the pasta in boiling water until *al dente*, rinse in cold water, and drain. Transfer to a serving bowl or platter and toss with the olive oil.

Chop the tomatoes coarsely. Pit and quarter the olives. Cut the goat cheese into ¼-inch chunks.

Mix the garlic and basil with the pasta. Then fold in the tomatoes, olives, and pine nuts. Sprinkle the salad with balsamic vinegar to taste, about 1–2 tablespoons. Add the cheese last and toss lightly. Garnish the salad with the chives and serve.

Artichoke Gnocci Salad

3–4 medium-size fresh artichokes (artichoke halves preserved in spring water or frozen artichokes may be substituted)
Lemon juice
Olive oil
½ pound dry gnocci or medium shells
⅓ cup Vinaigrette (page 40)
½ pound Gorgonzola or Roquefort cheese
⅓ cup chopped pistachios or walnuts
Freshly ground black pepper

Yield: 6–8 servings

This combination of artichokes, Gorgonzola, and pistachios can be served as a dinner salad, either before or after the main course.

To prepare the artichokes, trim the outer leaves and stems. Cut off ½ inch at the top of each artichoke. Arrange the artichokes upright in a deep saucepan, just large enough to hold them. Cover with boiling water and add a dash of lemon juice and a few drops of olive oil to the water to retain the fresh green color. Cook over medium heat for 30–45 minutes, or until the artichoke base is pierced easily with a fork through the top of the artichoke. Lift the artichokes out of the water and turn them upside down to drain. Halve or quarter the drained artichokes, depending on their size. Discard the inedible outer leaves.

Cook the gnocci in boiling water until *al dente*. Rinse in cold water, drain. Transfer to a serving bowl and toss with the dressing.

Add the artichokes to the gnocci and mix gently. Slice the cheese into ¼-inch chunks and add it to the salad. Sprinkle the nuts on top. Grind black pepper to taste over the salad and serve immediately.

Eggplant Fusilli Salad

½ pound dry fusilli
1 tablespoon virgin olive oil
1 large eggplant
1½ cups water
⅓ cup virgin olive oil
Juice of 1 lemon
½ teaspoon freshly ground black pepper
1 garlic clove, minced
1 sprig parsley
1 tablespoon fresh thyme or 1 teaspoon dried thyme
½ cup coarsely chopped red onion
¼ cup French Dressing (page 39)

Yield: 8–10 side dish servings

Cook the pasta in boiling water until *al dente*, rinse in cold water, drain. Transfer to a large serving bowl and toss with 1 tablespoon olive oil. Set aside.

Peel and cube the eggplant. In a saucepan, mix together the water, the remaining ⅓ cup olive oil, lemon juice, pepper, garlic, parsley, and the thyme. Bring to a boil and simmer for 5 minutes. Add the eggplant and cook for 10–15 minutes, or until the eggplant is tender. Allow the eggplant to cool in this sauce. Drain off the liquid from the eggplant and discard. Chill the eggplant for about 30 minutes.

Add the red onion and the dressing to the pasta and toss well. Then add the eggplant, toss gently, and serve.

Spiced Orzo Salad

½ pound dry orzo (rosamarina)
1 tablespoon virgin olive oil
¼ cup finely chopped fresh parsley
2 teaspoons finely chopped fresh cilantro
½ cup golden raisins
½ cup dried apricot halves, quartered
2–3 scallions, thinly sliced
2 tablespoons fresh ginger juice (squeezed from a 3–4-inch piece of fresh ginger with a garlic press)
Juice of 1 lemon
Freshly ground black pepper
Cilantro leaves

Yield: 8–10 side dish servings

This salad has an exotic combination of ingredients and a sweet and sour flavor. Serve it as a side to a curry dish.

Cook the orzo in boiling water for about 6 minutes. Rinse in cold water and drain well. Transfer to a serving bowl or platter and toss with the olive oil, parsley, and chopped cilantro.

Add the raisins, apricots, and scallions to the pasta. Combine the ginger juice with the lemon juice and toss with the salad. Grind black pepper to taste over the salad. Garnish with cilantro leaves and serve.

Note

The orzo tends to absorb the dressing readily and may need to be dressed with more lemon and ginger juice before serving.

Greek Orzo Salad

½ pound dry orzo (rosamarina)
1 tablespoon olive oil
2 medium-size firm tomatoes
¼ cup virgin olive oil
2 tablespoons lemon juice
¾ cup finely chopped fresh parsley
¼ cup finely chopped fresh mint
¼ cup minced red onion
Freshly ground black pepper

Yield: 8–10 side dish servings

This minty salad is similar to the Middle Eastern tabouli.

Cook the orzo in boiling water for about 6 minutes, or until *al dente*. Rinse in cold water and drain well. Transfer to a serving bowl and toss with 1 tablespoon olive oil.

Score, then blanch the tomatoes in boiling water for 30 seconds to loosen the skins. Peel, halve, and seed under running water. Pat dry and chop into ¼-inch chunks.

In a small bowl, whisk the remaining ¼ cup olive oil with the lemon juice and set aside.

Add the parsley, mint, and red onion to the orzo. Add the olive oil and lemon mixture and toss well. Gently stir in the tomatoes. Chill the salad for 1 hour.

If necessary, add more olive oil and lemon juice to the salad before serving. Grind black pepper to taste over the salad and serve.

Gingered Vegetable Penne Salad

½ pound dry penne or mostaccioli
1 tablespoon sesame oil
⅓–½ pound fresh snow peas
2 tablespoons peanut or other vegetable oil
1 large red bell pepper
5–6 fresh or canned water chestnuts (optional)
2 medium-size carrots
2-inch piece fresh ginger root
Juice of 1 lemon
1 teaspoon sugar
1–2 tablespoons water

Yield: 4–6 servings

This Japanese-style salad is a colorful combination of vegetables in a light ginger dressing.

Cook the pasta in boiling water until *al dente*, rinse in cold water, and drain. Transfer to a mixing bowl and toss with 1 tablespoon sesame oil.

Cut off the ends and strings from the snow peas. Heat the remaining 2 tablespoons peanut oil in a sauté pan. Add the snow peas and sauté until just translucent, 1–2 minutes. Drain on a paper towel.

Julienne slice the red bell pepper.

Peel and thinly slice the fresh water chestnuts. If you are using canned water chestnuts, rinse them first, then blanch them for 1 minute in boiling water. Drain and slice.

Slice the carrots on the diagonal into ¼-inch slices. Blanch the carrots in boiling water until tender crisp, 2–3 minutes. Refresh in cold water to stop further cooking and drain.

Toss the vegetables and water chestnuts with the cooked pasta. Peel the ginger, cut into chunks, and using a garlic press, squeeze out 2–3 tablespoons of ginger juice. Mix the ginger juice with the lemon juice, sugar, and water. Toss this mixture with the salad and serve.

Peanut-Sesame Cellophane Noodles

2 tablespoons light soy sauce
2 tablespoons water
1½ tablespoons smooth unsalted peanut butter
1 tablespoon tahini (sesame seed paste)
1½ tablespoons rice wine vinegar
1 tablespoon sesame oil
1 teaspoon chili oil
1 teaspoon sugar
1 teaspoon minced green onion or scallion
1 teaspoon minced garlic
1 teaspoon minced fresh ginger root
6 ounces cellophane noodles
2 cups fresh mixed vegetables (snow peas, thinly sliced carrots, peeled and diced cucumbers, bean sprouts, thinly sliced radishes, thinly sliced water chestnuts)
1 tablespoon sesame seeds
¼ cup unsalted roasted peanuts

Yield: 6–8 servings

In a small bowl, mix the soy sauce, water, peanut butter, tahini, vinegar, sesame oil, chili oil, sugar, green onion, garlic, and ginger root into a creamy brown paste. Set aside.

Cover the cellophane noodles with hot water and let them soak for 1 hour. Drain.

Combine the peanut-sesame sauce with the noodles and toss gently. Spread the vegetables over the top of the salad and sprinkle with sesame seeds and peanuts. Serve immediately.

Whole Wheat Health Salad

2 tablespoons sesame oil
1 tablespoon honey
2 tablespoons white wine vinegar or champagne vinegar
½ pound dry fettuccine or ¾ pound fresh whole wheat fettuccine (page 36), cut in 1½-inch pieces
3 medium-size carrots, grated
¼ cup unsalted sunflower seeds
¼ cup raisins or currants
¼ cup unsalted roasted peanuts
¼ cup chopped walnuts
¼ cup carob chips
¼ cup grated unsweetened raw coconut

Yield: 6–8 servings

This salad tastes similar to granola or to trail mix. Serve it as a nutritious snack.

In a small bowl, make the honey sesame dressing by combining the sesame oil, honey, and vinegar. The dressing tends to separate so be sure to mix it well before adding it to the pasta. Set aside.

Cook the pasta in boiling water until *al dente*, rinse in cold water, and drain. Transfer to a serving bowl and toss with the dressing.

Add the grated carrots, sunflower seeds, raisins, peanuts, walnuts, carob chips, and coconut to the pasta and toss well. Serve.

Dessert Pasta Salad

- ¼ cup honey
- ¼ cup golden rum, Triple Sec, or orange juice
- 1 teaspoon grated lime peel
- 2 tablespoons fresh lime juice
- 1 tablespoon chopped crystallized ginger (optional)
- ¾ cup fresh lemon linguine (page 34) or egg linguine (pages 23–26)
- 1½–2 cups bite-size fresh seasonal fruit (raspberries, strawberries, peaches, apricots, or melons)
- Fresh mint leaves

Yield: 6–8 servings

This salad combines fresh fruit with a sweet and sour dressing.

In a small bowl, make the dressing by combining the honey, rum, grated lime peel, lime juice, and the crystallized ginger. Set aside.

Cook the linguine in boiling water until *al dente*. Fresh linguine cooks in about 45 seconds. Rinse in cold water and drain. Transfer to a serving bowl. Mix with the dressing.

Toss the fruit with the pasta. Garnish the salad with fresh mint leaves. Serve at once.

5
Seafood Pasta Salads

Angels' Hair Caviar

¼ pound dry or ½ pound fresh angels' hair pasta or capellini
⅓ cup Lemon Vinaigrette (page 43)
⅓ pound fresh black or golden caviar
2 tablespoons thinly sliced fresh chives
4–6 teaspoons sour cream

Yield: 4–6 appetizers

This pasta salad is extremely delicate and each serving must be prepared individually.

Cook the pasta in boiling water until *al dente*. Dry pasta will cook in about 1 minute; fresh pasta will cook in about 15 seconds. Rinse immediately in cold water and drain. Shake out any excess water and toss with the dressing.

Divide the pasta among the individual serving plates. Spoon equal amounts of caviar onto each plate of pasta, and lightly fold the caviar into the pasta. Reserve a small amount of caviar for the garnish.

Dot the center of each salad with a teaspoon of sour cream, then place a little caviar on top. Sprinkle the salad with the chives and serve immediately.

Fettuccine With Smoked Salmon & Mushrooms

¾ pound fresh spinach fettuccine (page 27) and egg fettuccine (pages 23–26)
1 tablespoon virgin olive oil
⅓ pound smoked salmon or lox
½ pound mushrooms, thinly sliced
Juice from 1 lemon
1 teaspoon finely chopped fresh tarragon
1 teaspoon fresh thyme leaves
2 teaspoons minced garlic
2–4 tablespoons Chardonnay vinegar
Thinly sliced fresh chives

Yield: 4–6 servings

Cook the pasta in boiling water until *al dente*. Fresh fettuccine cooks in about 1 minute. Rinse in cold water and drain. Transfer to a mixing bowl and toss with the olive oil.

Slice the salmon into bite-size pieces. Briefly soak the mushrooms in lemon juice to prevent them from discoloring. Then drain.

Toss the pasta with the tarragon, thyme, and the garlic. Mix in the salmon and the mushrooms. Sprinkle the salad lightly with the Chardonnay vinegar to taste. Transfer to a serving platter, garnish with the chives, and serve.

Ligurian Pasta Salad

½ pound dry spaghetti rings
1 tablespoon virgin olive oil
2 large potatoes
2 anchovy fillets
⅓ cup Italian Dressing (page 38)
2 medium-size firm tomatoes
¼–⅓ pound green beans
1 large red bell pepper
6–8 Ligurian or Kalamata olives
1 can (4 ounces) water-packed tuna
2 teaspoons chopped capers

Yield: 4–6 servings

This salad makes a hearty meal.

Cook the pasta in boiling water until *al dente*, rinse in cold water, and drain. Transfer to a serving bowl and toss with the olive oil.

Peel and slice the potatoes into ¼-inch-thick slices. Steam until tender but still firm, about 6 minutes; do not overcook. Rinse the potatoes in cold water to stop further cooking and remove all the starch. Drain well. Cut the potatoes in half and set aside in a small bowl.

Soak the anchovy fillets in water to remove excess salt. Pat dry and chop finely.

Mix the anchovies with the potatoes. Toss with the dressing and set aside to marinate.

Score, then blanch the tomatoes in boiling water for 30 seconds. Peel, halve, and seed under running water. Pat dry and slice into thin wedges.

Slice the green beans on the diagonal into 1½-inch pieces. Blanch in boiling water for about 2 minutes. Refresh in cold water to stop further cooking. Drain.

Julienne slice the red bell pepper. Pit and quarter the olives. Coarsely chop the tuna.

Add the green beans, red bell pepper, olives, tuna, and capers to the pasta. Pour off the dressing from the potatoes and mix with the salad. Then add the potatoes and anchovies to the salad and toss well. Add the tomatoes last; toss gently and serve.

Mixed Seafood Pasta Salad

¼ cup dry small shells
¼ cup dry medium shells
1 tablespoon virgin olive oil
1 green bell pepper, julienne sliced
1 yellow bell pepper, julienne sliced
1 red bell pepper, julienne sliced
6–8 Greek olives, quartered
6–8 spicy Italian green olives, quartered
1–1½ pounds mixed fresh seafood (shrimp, prawns, clams, scallops, mussels)
2–3 tablespoons virgin olive oil
⅓ cup Lemon-Herb Dressing (page 47)

Yield: 4–6 servings

A spicy seafood salad with multi-colored bell peppers!

Cook the pastas separately in boiling water until *al dente*, rinse in cold water, and drain. Combine them in a mixing bowl and toss with 1 tablespoon of the olive oil. Add the peppers and the olives to the pasta and set aside.

Choose among the seafoods listed above. Poach shrimp in simmering water for about 5 minutes, then peel and devein. Shell, devein, and remove the tails from prawns. Brush prawns and scallops with olive oil and broil them close to the flame in a 500° F. oven for 3–5 minutes, turning once as the prawns turn pink and the scallops turn an opaque white. Remove them from the oven and drain on paper towels.

Steam the clams and mussels in their shells in a covered pan until the shells open. Detach the meat from the shells, rinse well to remove any sand particles, and drain.

Add all of the seafood to the pasta, sprinkle the salad with the dressing, and serve on a platter.

Anchovy Tagliarini Salad

½ pound dry spaghetti or ¾ pound fresh tagliarini
1 tablespoon virgin olive oil
4–5 anchovy fillets
2–3 tablespoons capers
¼–⅓ cup finely chopped fresh parsley
3–4 tablespoons coarsely chopped roasted red pepper
Parsley sprigs

Yield: 8–10 side dish servings

Cook the pasta in boiling water until *al dente*. Fresh tagliarini takes less than 30 seconds to cook. Rinse in cold water and drain. Transfer to a serving bowl and toss with the olive oil.

Soak the anchovies in water to eliminate excess salt, rinse, pat dry, and mince. Mince the capers if they are a large variety. If they are small, leave them intact.

Add the parsley to the pasta and mix well. Add the anchovies, then the capers, and finally the roasted pepper, tossing the salad with each addition. Garnish the salad with sprigs of parsley and serve.

Tuna Pasta Salad

½ pound dry wagon wheels or bowties
1 tablespoon virgin olive oil
1 can (8 ounces) water-packed albacore tuna
1–2 tablespoon capers
6–8 sun-dried tomatoes marinated in olive oil
2 tablespoons chopped fresh parsley
½–¾ cup fresh or frozen peas
Parsley sprigs

Yield: 4–6 servings

Cook the pasta in boiling water until *al dente*, rinse in cold water, and drain. Transfer to a serving bowl and toss with the olive oil.

Drain the tuna and chop coarsely. Mince the capers if they are large; keep them whole if they are small. Chop the tomatoes into bite-size pieces.

Toss the pasta first with the parsley, then with the capers, tomatoes, and the peas. Add the tuna last and mix it just enough to distribute it. Garnish the salad with parsley sprigs and serve.

Ceviche Pasta Salad

¾ pound fresh spinach linguine (page 27) and egg linguine (pages 23–26)
1 tablespoon virgin olive oil
½ pound fresh scallops
½ pound fresh sea bass, red snapper, or firm-fleshed sole fillet
Juice of 3 lemons
Juice of 1 lime
Juice of 1 orange
1 sweet red bell pepper
2 California or Anaheim green chile peppers
1 jalapeño pepper
2–3 tablespoons chopped fresh parsley
1½ teaspoons chopped fresh cilantro (optional)
1–2 tablespoons Chardonnay vinegar
3–4 tablespoons olive oil
2–3 teaspoons Dijon-style mustard
Freshly ground black pepper
1–2 avocados

Yield: 4–6 servings

This crisp and colorful seafood salad is marinated in lemon, lime, and orange juices. Serve it as a luncheon salad or as a first course for dinner.

Cook the pasta in boiling water for 45 seconds, rinse in cold water, drain. Transfer to a mixing bowl and toss with 1 tablespoon olive oil.

Cut large scallops into uniform-size pieces. Cut the fish fillet into bite-size pieces. Combine the raw fish and scallops with the lemon, lime, and orange juices in a nonmetallic nonplastic bowl. Set in the refrigerator to marinate until the fish turns an opaque white, 1–2 hours.

Julienne slice the bell pepper. Seed and finely chop the hot peppers.

Add the parsley, cilantro, and peppers to the pasta and toss well.

Make the dressing by combining the Chardonnay vinegar with the remaining 3–4 tablespoons olive oil and the mustard. Toss with the salad. Transfer the salad to a serving platter.

When the fish is ready, drain and discard the juice. Add the fish to the salad. Grind black pepper over the top, garnish the salad with thin slices of avocado, and serve immediately. Discard any remaining salad after 4–5 hours.

Pacific Coast Crab Salad

½ pound dry penne or mostaccioli
1 tablespoon virgin olive oil
2–3 pounds cracked fresh crab or 2 cups crabmeat
1 pound fresh asparagus
Juice of 2 lemons
2-inch piece fresh ginger root
1 teaspoon sugar
1 tablespoon prepared mustard
1 tablespoon mayonnaise
1–2 teaspoons prepared horseradish or fresh horseradish mixed with vinegar

Yield: 4–6 servings

This is a light seafood salad with a hint of ginger and a touch of horseradish.

Cook the pasta in boiling water until *al dente*, rinse in cold water, and drain. Transfer to a serving platter and toss with the olive oil.

Pull apart all the crabmeat and set aside. Cut off the inedible ends of the asparagus. Steam the asparagus until tender but crisp, 2–3 minutes. Cut the asparagus spears into 2-inch pieces. Slice the remaining stems of the asparagus into ¼-inch pieces. Marinate the asparagus in the lemon juice until ready to use.

Place the crabmeat in the center of the pasta. Drain the asparagus and reserve the lemon juice for the dressing. Place the asparagus in a decorative pattern around the crab.

Peel and cut the ginger into chunks. Squeeze out about 2 tablespoons of the ginger juice through a garlic press. Mix the juice with the sugar and the lemon juice. Toss gently with the salad.

Mix the mustard, mayonnaise, and the horseradish together. Use as a dipping sauce for the crab and asparagus.

Chill the salad and serve with the dipping sauce on the side.

Squid & Tomatillo Salsa Pasta Salad

5 tomatillos, fresh if possible
2 garlic cloves
1 California or Anaheim green chile pepper, seeded, stemmed, and cut into 1-inch pieces
1 jalapeño pepper, seeded, stemmed, and cut into 1-inch pieces
1–2 tablespoons fresh cilantro leaves
2 tablespoons chopped red onion
1–1½ pounds fresh squid (calamari)
½ pound dry small shells
1 tablespoon virgin olive oil
1 lemon, sliced

Yield: 4–6 servings

This is a spicy, fresh seafood salad with a South of the Border flavor.

To make the salsa, use a blender or food processor. Quarter the tomatillos and blend with the garlic, hot peppers, and cilantro, reserving a few leaves for a garnish. When this mixture is finely minced, add the onion and process briefly to distribute it. Set aside. The salsa can be made up to 1 day ahead.

Clean the squid by removing the head just below the eyes. Remove the ink sac intact if possible. Reserve the tentacles. Pull out the long featherlike transparent shell from the center of the body. Then rinse the inside of the body to remove the gelatinous matter. Cut the squid into ¼-inch rings. Bring a large pot of water to a rapid boil.

Add the squid, including the tentacles all at once. Cook for about 1 minute. Drain immediately. Pour the hot, drained squid into the bowl containing the salsa. Marinate for up to 1 hour.

Cook the pasta in boiling water until *al dente*, rinse it in cold water and drain well. Transfer the pasta to a serving bowl and toss it with the olive oil. Add the squid and the salsa to the pasta and mix well. Garnish the salad with fresh cilantro leaves and lemon slices and serve.

Broccoli & Prawn Linguine Salad

¾ pound fresh egg linguine (pages 23–26)
1 tablespoon virgin olive oil
1 dozen fresh jumbo prawns
2–3 tablespoons virgin olive oil
1 teaspoon fresh thyme leaves
1 teaspoon fresh tarragon leaves
3–4 garlic cloves, minced
4 broccoli stalks
⅓–⅔ cup Vinaigrette (page 40) or Caper Vinaigrette (page 41)

Yield: 4–6 servings

Serve this simple and elegant dish as an appetizer or as a first course.

Cook the pasta in boiling water until *al dente*; fresh linguine takes about 45 seconds. Rinse in cold water and drain. In a mixing bowl, toss with the olive oil.

Shell and devein the prawns, leaving the tail intact. Brush the prawns generously with the remaining 2–3 tablespoons olive oil, the thyme, tarragon, and garlic. Broil them close to the flame in a 500° F. oven, turning once, so they turn pink on both sides. Remove from the oven and let cool.

Chop off the inedible stems of the broccoli and discard. Steam the florets until tender crisp, 5–7 minutes. Refresh in cold water to prevent further cooking. Drain well and cut into attractive bite-size pieces.

Divide the pasta evenly among 4–6 medium-size plates. Place the broccoli and prawns decoratively in the pasta. Sprinkle each serving with the dressing. Serve.

Gingered Linguine With Clams

¾ pound fresh egg linguine (pages 23–26) or ¼ pound dry medium shells and ¼ pound dry small shells
1 tablespoon virgin olive oil
2 cups shucked tiny clams
3 tablespoons coarsely chopped red onion
1½ teaspoons chopped fresh cilantro or parsley
1–2 teaspoons minced fresh ginger root
⅓–½ cup pine nuts
Juice from 1 lemon
Freshly ground black pepper

Yield: 4–6 servings

Cook the linguine for about 45 seconds in boiling water. If you use the shells, cook them separately. Rinse the pasta in cold water, drain. Transfer to a serving dish and toss with the olive oil.

Drain and rinse the clams to remove the excess salt.

Reserve a little of the onion and some cilantro leaves for a garnish.

Add the clams, onion, cilantro, ginger root, and pine nuts to the pasta. Add the lemon juice and the black pepper to taste. Garnish the salad with the reserved red onion and cilantro leaves. Serve immediately; this salad does not keep well.

6
Pasta Salads With Chicken and Meats

Pesto Pasta Chicken Salad

½ pound dry creste di gallo, fusilli, rotelle, or cavatappi
1 tablespoon virgin olive oil
2 medium-size zucchini
¾–1 cup pesto (see Pesto Pasta Salad, pages 66–67)
2 cups shredded cooked chicken
1 cup cherry tomatoes, halved if large
1–2 tablespoons white wine vinegar (optional)
¼ cup pine nuts

Yield: 4–6 servings

Cook the pasta in boiling water until *al dente*, rinse in cold water, drain. Transfer to a serving bowl and toss with the olive oil.

Cut the raw zucchini into thin lengthwise strips about 1½ inches long and ¼ inch wide. Blanch in boiling water for 30–60 seconds, or until tender but firm. Refresh in cold water to stop further cooking. Drain well.

Add several large tablespoons of pesto to the pasta and mix thoroughly. Then add the chicken, zucchini, and the tomatoes. Add more pesto if necessary. If desired, add white wine vinegar to taste. Sprinkle the salad with pine nuts. Serve immediately.

Chicken Almond Curry Pasta Salad

½ pound dry or ¾ pound fresh spinach fettuccine (page 27) or hot red pepper fettuccine (page 35) or ½ pound dry rigatoni
1 tablespoon virgin olive oil
1½–2 teaspoons curry powder
½ teaspoon crushed red pepper flakes (use ¼ teaspoon if hot red pepper fettuccine is being used)
2½–3 cups cooked shredded chicken
1 small red bell pepper, julienne sliced
¼ cup almond slivers
¼ cup golden raisins
2–4 tablespoons Major Grey's mango chutney
⅓ cup unsweetened coconut shavings

Yield: 4–6 servings

In this hot and spicy Indian-style salad, lamb may be used in place of the chicken.

Cook the pasta in boiling water until *al dente*, rinse in cold water, and drain. Transfer to a mixing bowl and toss with the olive oil, curry powder, and hot red pepper.

Add the chicken, bell pepper, almonds, and raisins to the pasta. Mix in enough chutney to produce a moist, cohesive consistency. Transfer to a serving bowl or platter, sprinkle with the coconut shavings and serve.

Sesame Chicken Pasta Salad

¾ pound fresh spinach linguine (page 27) or egg linguine (pages 23–26)
1 tablespoon sesame oil
2 tablespoons coarsely chopped fresh cilantro
½ pound fresh mushrooms, thinly sliced
Juice from 1 lemon
⅓ pound fresh snow peas
1–2 teaspoons peanut or vegetable oil
1 red bell pepper
2–2½ cups shredded cooked chicken
⅓ cup cashews
⅓ cup Oriental Sesame Dressing (page 51)
1 tablespoon toasted sesame seeds

Yield: 4–6 servings

This light and crispy salad is an ideal meal in itself. Serve it for lunch or dinner.

Cook the pasta in boiling water until *al dente*, about 45 seconds. Rinse in cold water and drain. Transfer to a serving platter and toss with the sesame oil and the cilantro.

Soak the mushrooms in lemon juice for 5–10 minutes to preserve their color. Drain and discard the juice.

Cut off the ends and strings from the snow peas.

In a sauté pan, heat the peanut oil. Add the snow peas and sauté over high heat for 1 minute, or until translucent. Drain the snow peas on a paper towel.

Julienne slice the bell pepper.

Add the chicken, vegetables, and cashews to the pasta. Sprinkle the salad with the dressing, garnish with toasted sesame seeds, and serve.

Note

To toast sesame seeds, place them in a dry skillet over high heat and stir constantly until golden brown, about 1–2 minutes. Remove from the pan immediately.

Hunan Ginger Chicken Pasta Salad

½ pound dry spaghetti rings or ¾ pound fresh spinach fettuccine (page 27)
⅔ cup Hunan Dressing (page 52)
3 chicken breasts
Soy sauce
1 medium-size cucumber
1 medium-size carrot
1–1½ cups bean sprouts
¼–⅓ cup unsalted dry roasted peanuts
2 tablespoons freshly sliced chives

Yield: 4–6 servings

Cook the pasta in boiling water until *al dente*. Fresh fettuccine cooks in about 1 minute. Rinse in cold water and drain. Transfer to a mixing bowl and toss with about ⅓ cup dressing.

Baste the chicken with soy sauce and broil until tender and crisp, about 10 minutes on each side. Cool completely and shred.

Peel the cucumber and slice lengthwise into 1½-inch pieces. Cut each piece into thin strips. Peel and grate the carrot. Rinse and drain the bean sprouts.

In a serving bowl or platter, combine the pasta with the chicken, cucumber strips, grated carrot, and the bean sprouts. Add the remaining ⅓ cup dressing and toss well. Sprinkle the salad with peanuts and chives and serve.

Oriental Noodle Salad

½ pound Japanese somen or soba noodles
1½–2-inch piece fresh ginger root
1 tablespoon peanut or vegetable oil
1½–2 cups smoked duck or chicken pieces
8–10 fresh or reconstituted dry shitake mushrooms
3 scallions, thinly sliced
1 tablespoon fresh cilantro leaves
¾ cup Orange-Ginger-Soy Dressing (page 53)
Cilantro leaves

Yield: 4–6 servings

The smoked duck or chicken can be purchased in Chinese markets.

Cook the noodles in plenty of boiling water for 4–5 minutes or until *al dente*. Rinse in cold water, drain, and set aside in a serving dish.

Slice the ginger into six 8¼-inch-thick slices. Heat the oil in a skillet. Add the ginger with the duck, mushrooms, scallions, and cilantro and sauté over medium heat. Cook until the mushrooms are tender, about 5 minutes. Then discard the ginger root and toss the contents of the pan with the noodles.

Add the dressing and mix well. This salad may be served warm or at room temperature. Garnish with cilantro leaves.

Louisiana Orzo Salad

½ pound orzo (rosamarina) or ¾ pound fresh black pepper fettuccine (page 31)
1 tablespoon virgin olive oil
¼ cup chopped fresh parsley
2 garlic cloves, minced
3 scallions, thinly sliced
3 large Italian sausages, sweet or hot
½ pound cooked shrimp or fresh prawns
1 large green bell pepper
1½ cups small cherry tomatoes
1½–2 cups cooked shredded chicken
⅔ cup New Orleans Dressing (page 55)
Parsley sprigs

Yield: 4–6 servings

Cook the pasta in boiling water until *al dente*. Orzo cooks in about 6 minutes; fresh fettuccine cooks in about 1 minute. Rinse in cold water and shake out the excess water. Transfer to a serving bowl and toss with the olive oil, parsley, garlic, and scallions.

To cook the sausages, prick the skins with a fork, put them in a skillet with water to cover, and bring to a boil. Reduce the heat and poach for 1 minute. Drain off the water, cut the sausages into ½-inch slices, and fry over medium heat in a dry skillet until well browned. Drain on paper towels.

If you are using prawns, shell and devein them. Broil close to the flame in a 500° F. oven until pink, 2–3 minutes per side.

Julienne slice the bell pepper. If the

cherry tomatoes are large, slice them in half.

Mix the sausage, chicken, shrimp, bell pepper, and tomatoes with the pasta. Toss the salad with the dressing. Garnish with sprigs of parsley and serve.

Costa del Sol Orzo Salad

3 medium-size firm tomatoes
1–2 tablespoons virgin olive oil
1 green bell pepper, coarsely chopped
2 California or Anaheim green chile peppers, seeded and coarsely chopped
1 medium-size yellow onion, coarsely chopped
1 tablespoon cumin seeds, ground in a mortar and pestle
2–3 spicy pork sausages
½ pound dry orzo (rosamarina)
1½–2 cups shredded cooked chicken
½ pound cooked shrimp
2–3 tablespoons sherry vinegar
2–3 tablespoons finely chopped parsley
1–2 tablespoons finely chopped cilantro (optional)

Yield: 4–6 servings

A spicy, Spanish-style main course dish with shrimp, pork sausage, and chicken, and seasoned with sherry vinegar and cumin.

Score, then blanch the tomatoes in boiling water for about 30 seconds to loosen the skins. Peel, halve, and seed the tomatoes under running water. Pat dry and chop coarsely.

Heat the olive oil in a skillet over medium heat. Add the green bell pepper, chile peppers, onion, and half of the cumin. Cook for about 5 minutes, then add the tomatoes and increase the heat. Continue to cook until the peppers lose their raw taste but are still crisp, 5–8 minutes. Remove from the heat.

To cook the sausages, prick the skins

with a fork, put them in a skillet with water to cover, and bring to a boil. Then reduce the heat and poach for 1 minute. Drain off the water. Cut the sausages into ¼-inch-thick slices and fry over medium heat in a dry skillet until both sides are brown. Drain the sausages on paper towels.

Cook the orzo in boiling water for about 6 minutes; be careful not to overcook. Rinse in cold water, drain, and toss with the sautéed vegetables. Add the sausage, chicken, and the shrimp. Sprinkle the salad with the sherry vinegar to taste. Add the remaining ground cumin and toss well. Fold in the parsley and cilantro and serve.

Brunch Pasta Salad

½ pound dry penne or mostaccioli
1 tablespoon virgin olive oil
4–6 large Italian sausages
6–8 slices bacon
¼ pound cheddar cheese (New York cheddar is recommended)
2 large potatoes
2 tablespoons olive oil
2 tablespoons chopped onion
2 teaspoons chopped garlic
2 tablespoons chopped fresh parsley
Freshly ground black pepper
1–2 firm tomatoes, cut into wedges

Yield: 4–6 servings

Several popular brunch items are combined to produce a main course salad.

Cook the pasta in boiling water until *al dente*, rinse in cold water, and drain. Transfer to a mixing bowl and toss with 1 tablespoon olive oil.

To cook the sausages, prick the skins with a fork, put them in a skillet with water to cover, and bring to a boil. Reduce the heat and poach for 1 minute. Drain off the water, cut the sausages into ½-inch-thick slices, and fry over medium heat in a dry skillet until well browned on both sides. Drain on paper towels.

Cook the bacon until well browned and crisp. Drain on paper towels, then break into bite-size pieces.

Cut the cheese into ¼-inch chunks.

Peel the potatoes, cut into bite-size cubes, and steam in a pot until tender but not mushy, about 6 minutes. Pull them out of the steamer immediately, and rinse in cold water to remove all starch and prevent further cooking. Drain.

Heat a small skillet over medium heat. Add the remaining 2 tablespoons olive oil and the onion. Cook until the onion is translucent. Add the potatoes and garlic, and sauté over high heat until flavors are well distributed, 5–8 minutes.

On a large platter, combine the pasta with the two-thirds of the parsley and black pepper to taste. Add the bacon, sausages and cheddar cheese, and mix well. Spoon the potato mixture over the top of the salad. Sprinkle the potatoes with the remaining parsley and more ground pepper, garnish the edges of the salad with tomato wedges, and serve.

Winter White Bean Salad

1 tablespoon butter
1 medium-size yellow onion, chopped
½ cup thinly sliced celery
1½–2 cups canned or cooked great northern white beans or small white beans, drained
2–3 garlic cloves, minced
½ pound dry miniature bowties (farfalline)
¼ cup French Dressing (page 39)
¼ cup finely chopped fresh parsley
4–5 slices crisply cooked bacon, crumbled

Yield: 6–8 servings

Melt the butter in a skillet. Add the onion and celery and sauté over medium heat until translucent, 5–8 minutes. Add the beans and simmer over low heat for about 10 minutes. Stir in the garlic just before removing the skillet from the heat.

Cook the pasta in plenty of boiling water until *al dente*, 2–3 minutes. Rinse in cold water and drain. Transfer to a serving bowl. Add the bean mixture and the dressing to the pasta and toss well.

Lightly toss the salad with the parsley and bacon and serve. This salad can be served warm or at room temperature.

Anti-Pasto Pasta Salad

½ pound dry spaghetti rings or creste di gallo
1 tablespoon virgin olive oil
6–8 sun-dried tomatoes marinated in olive oil
6 artichoke hearts, canned in spring water and drained or frozen and defrosted
¼ pound dry salami, sliced ¼-inch thick
¼ pound Fontina cheese
8 spicy green Italian olives
4 mild marinated cherry peppers
4 hot marinated cherry peppers
4 hot marinated pepperocini peppers
⅓ cup Italian Dressing (page 38) or Caper Vinaigrette (page 41)

Yield: 8–10 side dish servings

This is an attractive, spicy salad that makes an impressive buffet item.

Cook the pasta in boiling water until *al dente*, rinse in cold water, and drain. Transfer to a serving bowl and toss with the olive oil.

Quarter the tomatoes, the artichoke hearts, and the salami slices. Cut the cheese into bite-size chunks. Halve and pit the olives, reserving a few whole ones for the garnish. Drain and slice the peppers into thin ringlets, reserving a few whole ones for the garnish.

Combine all the ingredients with the pasta and toss with the dressing. Garnish the salad with whole olives and peppers and serve.

Chardonnay Vinaigrette Rotelle Salad

½ pound dry egg or spinach rotelle
1 tablespoon virgin olive oil
2–3 garlic cloves, minced
½ pound salami, cubed
½ cup chopped walnuts
2–3 tablespoons coarsely chopped roasted red peppers
2–3 scallions, thinly sliced
½ cup Chardonnay Vinaigrette (page 44)
¼ cup grated Pecorino Romano cheese

Yield: 4–6 servings

This salad is wonderful for picnics.

Cook the rotelle in boiling water until *al dente*, rinse in cold water, and drain well. Transfer to a serving bowl and toss with the olive oil and garlic.

Add the salami, walnuts, peppers, and scallions to the pasta.

Toss the dressing with the salad. Sprinkle the cheese over the salad and serve.

Three Cheese Deli Salad

½ pound dry creste di gallo or macaroni
1 tablespoon virgin olive oil
¼ pound mozzarella cheese
¼ pound Asiago cheese
¼ pound sharp cheddar
¼ pound dry salami
2 anchovy fillets
1 tablespoon minced garlic
½ teaspoon chopped capers
2 scallions, thinly sliced
¼ cup pine nuts
⅓ cup Italian Dressing (page 38)

Yield: 8–10 side dish servings

The 3 distinctively different cheeses, one mild, one spicy, and one sharp, make this salad unique.

Cook the pasta in boiling water until *al dente*, rinse in cold water, and drain well. Transfer to a serving bowl and toss with the olive oil.

Cut the cheeses and salami into ½-inch chunks. Drain the anchovy fillets, pat dry, and chop finely.

Add the garlic, capers, and anchovies to the pasta and toss well. Then add the cheeses, salami, scallions, and pine nuts.

Toss the dressing with the salad and serve.

San Fransisco Pasta Salad

1½–2 cups fresh watercress leaves (15–20 sprigs)
⅓–½ pound pancetta (Italian bacon), sliced paper thin
½ pound dry rotelle
½ cup Raspberry Walnut Vinaigrette (page 45)
½ pound chèvre (goat cheese), cut in ¼-inch chunks
Fresh sliced chives
2 ripe bosc or comice pears, peeled and sliced

Yield: 6–8 side dish servings

San Francisco is currently the center of the fashionable California Cuisine, a new style of cooking that combines a variety of ethnic foods with fresh fruits, vegetables, and meats. The following is my contribution.

Wash and trim the stems from the watercress. Pat the leaves dry, wrap in a dish towel, and return to the refrigerator to become crisp.

Fry or microwave the pancetta until crisp, as you would bacon. Drain on paper towels and wipe off excess grease.

Cook the pasta in boiling water until *al dente*, rinse in cold water, and drain.

Decoratively cover a serving platter with the watercress. Mound the cooked pasta in the center of the platter. Pour the dressing over the pasta. Lightly toss the pancetta with the pasta. Distribute the cheese across the top of the salad. Sprinkle the chives over the cheese. Garnish the sides of the platter with the pears. Toss the salad gently before serving.

Variation

Use Gorgonzola cheese in place of the chèvre.

Martini Pasta Salad

½ pound dry small shells
1 tablespoon virgin olive oil
1 cup fresh green beans
½ cup green martini olives
2–3 tablespoons chopped roasted red pepper
¼ cup whole raw almonds
¼ cup Martini Dressing (page 46)
⅓–½ pound cooked ham, cubed

Yield: 4–6 servings

Cook the shells in boiling water until *al dente*. Rinse in cold water, drain. Transfer to a serving bowl and toss with the olive oil.

Blanch the green beans in boiling water for 1–2 minutes, refresh in cold water to stop further cooking, drain, and slice into 1-inch pieces. Halve the olives. Coarsely chop the pepper. Reserve a few almonds for a garnish and slice the rest lengthwise into slivers. Toast in a dry frying pan over high heat for 3–5 minutes. Be careful not to burn them.

Make the dressing and toss well with the pasta. Add all the other ingredients individually to the salad, mixing gently with each addition. Garnish with the reserved toasted almonds and serve.

Hawaiian Summer Sea Shell Salad

½ cup fresh orange juice
1 tablespoon grated orange rind
½ cup sunflower or other vegetable oil
¼ teaspoon ground cloves
Freshly ground black pepper
½ pound dry small shells
1–2 cups fresh or unsweetened canned pineapple, cut in 1-inch pieces
2 oranges, sectioned and cut bite-size
⅓ pound cooked ham, julienne sliced
1 green bell pepper, julienne sliced
1 red bell pepper, julienne sliced
2 medium-size carrots, very thinly sliced on the diagonal
¼ cup fresh or frozen peas
⅓ cup macadamia nuts (unsalted)
¼ cup unsweetened raw coconut flakes

Yield: 4–6 servings

Imagine yourself on a sandy beach on a tropical island with a refreshing pasta salad and a cool drink.

Make the dressing by mixing the orange juice with the orange rind, sunflower oil, cloves, and freshly ground pepper to taste.

Cook the pasta in boiling water until *al dente*, rinse in cold water, and drain. Transfer to a serving platter and toss with the dressing.

Add the pineapple, oranges, ham, bell peppers, carrots, and peas to the salad. Garnish the salad with the macadamia nuts and coconut flakes. Serve immediately.

Middle East Orzo Salad

2 medium-size firm tomatoes
1–2 tablespoons virgin olive oil
1 medium-size onion, coarsely chopped
1 sweet green bell pepper, coarsely chopped
2 medium-size carrots, diagonally sliced ¼-inch thick
½ pound dry orzo (rosamarina)
3 garlic cloves, minced
¼ cup finely chopped fresh parsley
2 cups cooked lamb, julienne sliced
1 can (14 ounces) garbanzo beans (chick-peas), drained and rinsed
¼ cup almond slivers
¼ cup pine nuts
¼ cup currants
½ medium-size cucumber, finely chopped
1 pint plain yogurt
1½ tablespoons finely chopped fresh mint
2–3 tablespoons fresh lemon juice
Parsley sprigs

Yield: 4–6 servings

An exotic mixture of fruits, nuts, vegetables, herbs, lamb, and yogurt.

Score, then blanch the tomatoes in boiling water for 30 seconds to loosen the skins. Peel, halve, and seed under running water. Pat dry. Chop coarsely.

Heat the olive oil in a skillet. Add the onion, green pepper, carrots, and tomatoes and sauté over medium heat until the onions are translucent and the pepper is tender-crisp. Set aside.

Cook the orzo in plenty of boiling water for about 6 minutes. Be careful not to overcook or it will become mushy. Rinse in cold water. Drain and transfer to a serving bowl. Add the sautéed vegetables to the orzo and mix well. Then add the garlic and parsley and mix again. Mix in the lamb, garbanzo beans, almonds, pine nuts, and currants.

Mix the cucumber with the yogurt and mint. Add lemon juice to taste. Toss the yogurt sauce with the salad and garnish with parsley sprigs. Serve immediately.

Slavic Macaroni Salad

3 medium-size beets
1 tablespoon virgin olive oil
1 tablespoon red wine vinegar
3 medium-size red potatoes
3 medium-size carrots
½ pound dry macaroni or ¾ pound fresh beet fettuccine (page 28)
1 tablespoon virgin olive oil
¼ cup Horseradish Dressing (page 56)
⅓–½ pound tender cooked beef, thinly sliced

Yield: 4–6 servings

This is a hearty main dish salad containing beets, carrots, potatoes, and beef in a spicy horseradish sauce.

Wash the beets well and cut off the tops, leaving 2 inches of stem. Boil until tender, about 20–30 minutes. Let the beets cool, then remove their skins. Julienne slice and combine with 1 tablespoon olive oil and the vinegar. Set aside to marinate.

Cut the potatoes into bite-size cubes. Steam until tender but firm. Check after 3–5 minutes; continue to cook if necessary. Rinse in cold water to prevent further cooking. Drain and set aside.

Cut the carrots into thin 1½-inch long strips. Blanch for about 30 seconds in boiling water, or until tender-crisp. Refresh in cold water to stop further cooking and drain.

Cook the macaroni in boiling water until *al dente*, rinse in cold water, drain. Transfer to a mixing bowl and toss with the remaining 1 tablespoon olive oil.

Add the potatoes and carrots to the pasta. Then add the dressing and toss well. Add the meat and mix lightly. Transfer to the mixing bowl. Keep the beets separate from the salad to prevent them from discoloring it. Just before serving, garnish individual servings of salad with the beets.

Japanese Beef & Noodle Salad

¼ cup soy sauce
2 tablespoons sugar
¼ cup dry sherry
2 garlic cloves, minced
½ lemon, thinly sliced
2 teaspoons grated fresh ginger root
12 ounces shell steak, cut in teriyaki strips, about ¾ inch by 2 inches
1 package (16 ounces) tofu
Soy sauce
Water
1 cup fresh bean sprouts
1 can (8 ounces) baby corn
1 tablespoon sesame oil
2 tablespoons rice wine vinegar
1 teaspoon Dijon-style mustard
½ pound dry or ¾ pound fresh spinach fettuccine (page 27)
Thinly sliced fresh chives

Yield: 4–6 servings

My aunt's sukiyaki inspired this recipe.

Make a marinade by mixing ¼ cup soy sauce, the sugar, sherry, garlic, lemon, and ginger in a nonmetallic bowl. Add the beef and marinate for up to 2 hours. Barbecue or broil the steak strips quickly over high heat until medium rare. Set aside.

Rinse the tofu, drain, and pat dry. Cut into 1-inch cubes. Fill a frying pan ¾ inch high with a 1 to 1 mixture of soy sauce and water, and heat to boiling. Add the tofu in a single layer, cover, and cook for about 3 minutes. Remove the tofu from the boiling liquid and drain on paper towels.

Wash and drain the bean sprouts. Drain the baby corn and rinse to remove excess salt.

Mix together the sesame oil, rice wine vinegar, and mustard to make a dressing.

Boil the pasta until *al dente*. Fresh fettuccine cooks in about 1 minute. Rinse in cold water and drain. Transfer to a serving bowl and toss with the dressing. Add the bean sprouts and corn to the pasta and toss. Then add the meat. Add the tofu last, being careful not to crumble it. Garnish the salad with the chives and serve.

Tangerine & Turkey Linguine Salad

¾ pound fresh egg linguine (pages 23–26) or ½ pound dry linguine
1 tablespoon virgin olive oil
2–3 tangerines
½ cup peeled and thinly sliced fresh or canned water chestnuts
2 cups shredded cooked turkey meat
2 cups thinly sliced celery
⅓–½ cup chopped walnuts
⅓ cup Lemon Vinaigrette (page 43) or ¼ cup Balsamic Vinaigrette (page 42)
Walnuts

Yield: 6–8 servings

This recipe was created for the day after Thanksgiving. The salad is best when it has marinated with the dressing in the refrigerator for several hours.

Cook the pasta in boiling water until *al dente*. Fresh linguine cooks in 45 seconds. Rinse in cold water, drain. Transfer to a serving bowl and toss with the olive oil.

Peel and section the tangerines, detach their membranes, and slice each section into thin slivers. If you are using canned water chestnuts, rinse them, blanch in boiling water for 1 minute, then drain.

Add the turkey, celery, tangerines, and water chestnuts to the pasta. Toss with the dressing. Garnish the salad with walnuts and serve.

Glossary of Ingredients

Asiago. A spicy and sharp Italian cheese made from cows' milk, asiago is sold in most Italian delicatessens and is used primarily for grating. Imported Parmesan may be substituted.

Basil. An historic herb native to the Far East, basil is famous as the basis of pesto in Italy and pistou in France. This leafy plant grows from April through September, so be sure to purchase it in season and preserve it in olive oil for use during the winter months.

Capers. These hand-picked flower buds of a desert shrub native to the Sahara are grown commercially in the Mediterranean region. Capers make a pungent addition to seafood, meat, and vegetable dishes.

Caviar. Caviar is actually fish eggs, or roe, from sturgeon. The best caviar is very fresh, lightly salted, crisp, and firm. Golden caviar comes from whitefish roe. Buy the caviar as fresh as possible, keep it refrigerated, and eat it immediately.

Cellophane Noodles. Made from the flour of mung beans, they are thin and white and transparent and are used in Chinese and Southeast Asian cooking. Soak them in hot water for about 1 hour, drain, and use.

Chèvre. A goats' milk cheese that has its origins in France, when fresh, chèvre is characterized by a tart flavor and chalky consistency. Firm chèvres, such as the French Montrachet, Bucheron, and Lezay, or California chèvre, are ideal cheeses to use in salads.

Chili Oil. A spicy bright red oil used to season oriental sauces, it is a mixture of ground chiles, vegetable oil, and salt.

Cilantro or Chinese Parsley. Also known as fresh coriander, cilantro is an herb common to Chinese, Middle Eastern, and Latin

American cooking. A member of the parsley family with a pungent citrus rind flavor, cilantro is an acquired taste for many. Fresh cilantro can be purchased all year long in many areas.

Cumin. This is a familiar spice to Mexican, South American, and Spanish cooking. For maximum flavor, purchase cumin seed and pulverize it in a mortar and pestle.

Feta. A dense white Greek cheese, feta has a salty, tangy flavor. In Greece, it is made from either goats', ewes' or cows' milk. Feta must be kept in water or brine to prevent it from spoiling. Denmark makes a similar cheese by the same name.

Fontina. Made from sheeps' milk cheese, this cheese has a delicate taste. It is made both in Italy and in Scandinavia and can be found in most supermarkets. I prefer Italian fontina for pasta salads.

Ginger. This gnarled root is spicy and aromatic when it is peeled and grated. Traditionally found in Chinese and Indian cuisine, it is used to flavor vegetables, beef, fish, fowl, and fruit.

Gorgonzola. Italy's famed blue cheese, Italian Gorgonzola varies from a well-aged strong cheese to the mild and sweet *dulce latte*. Our domestic Gorgonzola, though less flavorful, is a fairly good substitute. Blue cheese or Roquefort can also be substituted.

Horseradish. A stringy root with a strong stinging flavor, horseradish goes well with cold meats. It is usually sold in a vinegar brine but you can purchase it fresh, then grate and mix it with vinegar.

Kalamata Olives. These slitted, purple-black, almond-shaped olives are produced in Greece. Kalamata olives have been soaked in salt brine and packed in red wine vinegar. Because they have a robust flavor, use them sparingly to avoid overpowering a salad.

Pancetta. Coming from the same cut of pork as bacon, pancetta is seasoned with salt and spices, then cured rather than smoked. It is more delicate tasting than bacon and should be sliced thinly and cooked crisply. Pancetta can be purchased at delicatessens. If you can't find pancetta, substitute proscuitto, unsmoked ham, or bacon that has been simmered in water for 10 minutes, drained, and rinsed with fresh cold water.

Parmigiano-Reggiano. This is the famous Parmesan cheese from the Enzo Valley between the towns of Parma and Reggio in Italy. This spicy, strong cheese is aged for 2 years, which gives it a flavor far superior to our mild domestic Parmesan. It can be purchased in most Italian delis.

Pecorino Romano. An extremely sharp and salty sheeps' milk cheese from Italy, Pecorino Romano can be very overpowering. It is best used in highly seasoned foods. Because domestic Romano is considerably milder and is more similar to domestic Parmesan, it is not a good substitute. It can be purchased at Italian delis.

Pine Nuts. These oily, slender nuts are the kernels from the cones of the stone or umbrella pine tree and are native to the Mediterranean countries and to China. They add a pleasant, subtle crunch to salads. Pine nuts can be found in most supermarkets, health food stores, and gourmet food shops.

Raspberry Vinegar. A good quality wine vinegar is combined with raspberry juice to make raspberry vinegar. It is found in most gourmet shops. Other fruit-flavored vinegars can be substituted for it.

Roasted Red Peppers. These are red bell peppers that have been charred and blistered over a fire. These charcoal-flavored peppers add color and zest to salads and antipasto dishes. Roasted red peppers are sold in most grocery stores; sometimes they are sold under the name "fire-roasted peppers." They can also be made at home using red bell peppers. Char the peppers under the broiler or over an open flame turning them until the skins blacken. Remove them from the heat, seal them in a paper bag, and let them steam for 10 minutes. Remove the skins and seeds, rinse and pat dry, cut the peppers into strips. Use them immediately or preserve them in vinegar brine.

Rice Wine Vinegar. Produced from the fermentation of rice, rice wine vinegar is lighter, milder, and less acidic than distilled vinegar. It makes a pleasant marinade in oriental-style salads. Although white, red, and black rice vinegars are made, the white rice vinegar is best for salads.

Sesame Oil. A golden oil made from sesame seeds, sesame oil provides the distinctive flavor characteristic of oriental foods. Cold-pressed sesame oil does not have the same flavor and should not be substituted. Oriental sesame oil can be purchased in oriental markets and some supermarkets.

Shitake Mushrooms. The oldest cultivated mushrooms, shitake mushrooms are a staple of Asian cooking. Fresh shitake mushrooms can be treated like any other mushroom. Dry ones must be reconstituted first by pouring boiling water over and soaking them for about 30 minutes.

Soba. A Japanese noodle made out of buckwheat flour, soba can be purchased in Japanese markets and at some large supermarkets. Whole wheat pasta can be substituted.

Somen. This is a Japanese, hardwheat noodle made out of buckwheat flour. If it is difficult to find, spaghetti noodles are a good substitute.

Sun-dried Tomatoes. Known as *pumate* in Italy, these pear shaped tomatoes have been halved and dried in the sun. They are usually preserved in olive oil. Commercial products tend to be salty, while homemade versions usually taste sweeter and can be dried in the oven or dehydrator with little or no salt. Sun-dried tomatoes add spice and intense flavor to salads.

Tahini. A paste made from sesame seeds, tahini has a consistency similar to peanut butter and is used in Middle Eastern dishes. It can usually be found in the health food section of the supermarket.

Tomatillo. This is a green tomatolike fruit that is covered with a brown paper husk. Tomatillos have a lemony flavor and can be as small as a walnut or as large as a lemon. They are common to Mexican cooking. Canned tomatillos can be substituted, although they tend to be very salty.

Water Chestnuts. These deep purplish-brown bulbs grow in muddy water. Although it can be time consuming to peel them, they are well worth the effort. Their crispness and their juicy, sweet flavor are a wonderful addition to salads and sautéed dishes. Water chestnuts are found primarily in oriental markets. Unfortunately, canned ones are a poor substitute. If you do substitute canned water chestnuts for fresh, be sure to rinse them, blanch them for 1 minute in boiling water, and drain well.

Index

D

E

F

G

N

O

P

R

S

T

V

W

Y

NOTES

NOTES

NOTES

NOTES

NOTES

OTHER COOKBOOKS FROM THE CROSSING PRESS

PESTOS! COOKING WITH HERB PASTES by Dorothy Rankin $7.95, 144 pages, 8x6

"It's an inventive and tasteful collection and it makes the possibilities of herb pastes so enticing one wonders why such a book hasn't appeared before now." (*Publishers Weekly*)

29 recipes for pesto from the classic basil pesto to the more unusual creamy tarragon pesto and sorrel pesto with lemon + 60 recipes for dishes using those pestos, including soups, appetizers, sauces for pasta, bread, marinades for grillling, salad dressings, and entrees.

SALSAS! by Andrea Chesman $7.95, 128 pages, 8x6

Written for all those who have found themselves addicted to the wonderful hot sauces of Mexico, South America, Central America and North Africa, this provides 20 original salsa recipes + 70 recipes for dishes using salsa as the main flavoring ingredient, from pasta salads to Buffalo-style chicken wings, from Mexican Chimichangas to Chinese Sesame Chicken to North African Couscous-Stuffed Eggplant.

CABBAGETOWN CAFE COOKBOOK by Julie Jordan $10.95, 256 pages, 8½x11

Imaginative, sure-fire recipes from the legendary Cabbagetown Cafe in Ithaca, New York. Julie took the restaurant recipes, cut them down to size and experimented with them to make sure they worked in the home kitchen. These are delicious and inventive vegetarian recipes. Over 170 recipes, from appetizers to entrees to desserts. The desserts chapter alone is worth the price of admission.

WINGS OF LIFE, VEGETARIAN COOKERY by Julie Jordan $8.95, 256 pages, 6x9

Our best selling cookbook, this is a classic vegetarian cookbook. No white sugar, no white flour. "Jordan's book shows a love of food and a willingness to experiment that mark creative cooking." (*The Library Journal*)

WHOLE GRAIN BAKING by Diana Scesny Greene $8.95, 200 pages, 6x9

"The more than 100 recipes for bread, biscuits, crackers, griddle cakes, pancakes and whole grain snacks are varied, appetizing, and clearly written." (*Publishers Weekly*)

At your local bookstore or write directly to The Crossing Press, Trumansburg, New York 14886. Please add $1.00 for postage on the first book, 50¢ for each additional book. Or write for a free catalog of our many cookbooks.